Children's
Television

Children's Television

The Art, the Business, and How It Works

Cy Schneider

foreword by
Fred Silverman

NTC Business Books
a division of National Textbook Company

Published by NTC Business Books, an imprint of
National Textbook Company, 4255 West Touhy Avenue,
Lincolnwood (Chicago) Illinois 60646-1975 U.S.A.
Manufactured in the United States of America.
Library of Congress Catalog Card Number: 87-60440

7 8 9 0 IB 9 8 7 6 5 4 3 2 1

Table of Contents

ILLUSTRATIONS AND TELEVISION COMMERCIAL STORYBOARDS

Illustrations

Television Commercial Storyboards

Foreword

NOBODY IS MORE QUALIFIED TO WRITE THE DEFINITIVE BOOK ABOUT THE BUSINESS and art of children's television than Cy Schneider. Whether you're a professional in the field or an interested parent, I'm certain you will find his thoughts and historical overview of the subject fascinating and informative, leading to a real understanding of the complexities and challenges of children's television in the '80s and beyond.

I first met Cy Schneider in 1964. He was in charge of the Mattel account at Carson/Roberts and the most influential buyer of children's programs in the United States. I was the recently appointed Director of Daytime Programs for CBS and was facing my first major crisis, the collapse of the network's once dominant Saturday morning schedule. Thanks to ABC's introduction of "The Beatles" cartoon series, CBS would have to scrap its entire children's lineup for the fall of 1964 and introduce eight new programs—all superhero shows. It was the most sweeping schedule change in the history of children's television, and the network faced its first real test. It had to get advertisers to endorse the schedule, and more importantly, buy it!

Cy Schneider called the shots for Mattel. His reaction, representing Saturday morning's largest advertiser, would either make or break the lineup, for the rest of the advertisers would follow his lead.

Cy really impressed me at that meeting. He listened intently to the presentation, and then asked *all* the right questions. He seemed to know as much about the shows as I did, as he probed me about the various character relationships, story direction, character design, and (would you believe it?) the superpowers of the Lone Ranger and Space Ghost! I could see that this was a serious business to him, and that nothing but the best would be good enough for his young constituents.

To my relief, Cy liked the new shows and Mattel bought heavily into them. And to our relief, the 1964, 1965 schedule went on to become an enormous success!

Through the rest of my tenure at CBS and later at ABC and NBC, our paths continued to cross. Cy and his associates at Carson/Roberts and Mattel were instrumental in launching such new series as "Scooby Doo: Where Are You?," the CBS "Children's Film Festival," "Archie," and "The Smurfs." I came to realize that Cy's group in California had the Midas touch when it came to picking hits. More importantly, Cy was a consummate professional with integrity—he really cared about young people as consumers and viewers. He would often say, "The best way to improve children's television is to begin communicating with children clearly, with honesty, sensitivity, and respect which they as the audience deserve." It is this philosophy that has led him to more than 30 years of outstanding achievements in the children's arena—from his early days with Mattel and the creation of Barbie to the launching of the Peabody Award-winning Nickelodeon cable network, which he pioneered at Warner-Amex.

I considered myself to be somewhat of an expert on children's television until I read Cy's book. Now I realize how little I really knew!

Fred Silverman

A Matter of Indebtedness

I OWE A DEBT OF THANKS TO AN INNUMERABLE NUMBER OF PEOPLE AND COMPAN-ies who made this book possible.

First, I would like to thank all of the following companies for allow-ing me to use illustrations of their copyrighted material: American Greet-ings; Children's Television Workshop; D.C. Comics Inc.; Edgar Rice Bur-roughs, Inc.; Filmation; General Foods Corporation; General Mills; Griffin Bacal Inc.; Hanna-Barbera Productions, Inc.; Hardee's Food Systems; Li-censing Corporation of America; Lorimar-Telepictures, Inc.; Mattel, Inc.; Nickelodeon; The Procter & Gamble Company; The Quaker Oats Com-pany; Tribune Media Services; Viewmaster Ideal Group, Inc.; and Walt Disney Productions.

For my 32 years of experience in working with children's television and children's advertising, I would like to thank the clients who hired me to do their advertising work, with a particular thanks to some of the wonderful people I worked with at those client companies: Mattel—Mike Arthur, Spencer Boise, Victor Cole, Josh Denhan, Paul Guggenheim, Ed Hamowy, Herb Holland, Cliff Jacobs, Jack Jones, Tom Kalinske, Bernie Loomis, Philippe Mayer, Art Spear, Ray Wagner, and most of all, Ruth and Elliot Handler, without whom this book would not have been possible; General Foods—Jim Ferguson, Jack Keenan, Kent Mitchell, Jim Tappan, and Steve Price; Universal Studios—Jay Stein and Herb Steinberg; Baskin-Robbins—Butch Baskin, Bruce Enderwood, and Irv Robbins. A particular kind of thanks to Dick Grey and Bob Lurie of Tyco Industries for bringing me and my associate, John La Pick, back into the toy industry.

And I extend my thanks to another group of companies with whom I did individual consulting projects: Hershey's, Lever, Nabisco Brands, and Ralston.

Because the Mattel story plays such a predominant role in this book and 26 years of my life, and because the work done for Mattel had such an impact on the history of children's television, I feel it is important to thank and credit the people at Carson/Roberts and Ogilvy & Mather who were my comrades in arms. These are the people who made the difference: Russ Alben, Tony Asher, Dick Chodkowski, Ken Clark, Dan Dixon, Margo Eldridge, Jim Frew, Tony Haller, Pat Heine, Dennis Higgins, Mary Louise Lau, Cynthia Lawrence, Paul Mimiaga, Jill Murray, Arthur Nissman, Dick Perkins, Betty Pumpian, Vel Rankin, George Rappaport, Leo Salkin, Pat Shields, Eddie Smardan, Ken Sullet, Bob Stewart, and Herb Yager.

Thanks to Ken Snyder for "The Funny Company" and so much more.

A very special thanks to Jack Schneider and John Lack for hiring me to manage Nickelodeon where I learned so much about creating and producing children's programming. I am in their debt for the opportunity and the autonomy to have created a rich body of award-winning children's television. Part of that thanks belongs to Steve Ross of Warner Communications and James Robinson III of American Express for the courage to fund the startup of Warner-Amex and Nickelodeon. Additional thanks go to the other people who made Nickelodeon a Peabody Award winner: Virgina Carter, Tippy Fortune, Don Herbert, Alice Myatt, Reggie Jackson, Bob Klein, Geraldine Laybourne, Fred Newman, Jeffrey Weber, and Roger Yager.

My most heartfelt debt must be paid to three men who took an interest in my career and taught me most of what I know about advertising: Andrew Kershaw, David Ogilvy, and Jack Roberts. For their constant encouragement to write this book, I must thank: the late Ralph Carson, Ken Roman, and my present colleagues, Chuck Peebler and David Bell.

A most singular thanks to Bernie Loomis who has been a client, a competitor, a friend, and an inspiration.

Thanks to Joanne Medeiros, Holiday Vaill, and Linda Brochert for typing the manuscript and coordinating the myriad details it takes to put a book like this together.

Most importantly, my thanks to my wife Jacqueline for so many things. Only she knows how many hours I stole from her and my family to get this book written.

This book is dedicated to Walt Disney, the greatest Pied Piper of them all.

It was written for my two-year old daughter, Alexandra, with the hope that she and the other children of her generation will have a rewarding childhood television watching experience.

DECEMBER 1986
LOS ANGELES, CALIFORNIA

CHAPTER 1

The First Guidebook to Children's Television

THIS BOOK IS THE FIRST PRACTICAL GUIDE TO THE BUSINESS AND ART OF CHILdren's television. It is also the first positive book about this subject.

I wrote it because no one else did. Or would, I suspect. Taking a positive view of children's television when its faults and problems have been so widely publicized might be viewed by some, I suspect, as inappropriate, yet the critical books and articles regarding children's television plus all the political clamor and parental complaints accompanying them have not been as constructive as one might hope. Because the literature has not found an audience among businessmen or practitioners of the art, the books and articles have been largely dismissed or ignored. Of the 3,000-odd articles written on children's television, particularly those published by social scientists, most are not written in a language easy for those outside of academia to understand. The journals that review the books or contain articles discussing research findings on children's television viewing are not even known to the people who work at the business or art of children's television.

This first guidebook then, is an effort to be more pragmatic. It takes another point of view, a practical and constructive one.

If children's television is to get better, to be more socially acceptable, those who work in it must practice their art and business with greater sensitivity, knowledge, and awareness of how children react to television. The best way to improve children's television is to begin communicating with children clearly, and with the honesty, sensitivity, and respect they deserve. We must stop treating children as helpless, gullible sheep who need to be carefully watched and protected. There is no evidence that television is the wolf in sheep's clothing that is slowly devouring our children, though many critics would have you believe that. Children are not that easy to entertain or persuade; they will not watch anything put in front of them on television, and will not buy (or ask to buy) everything that is cleverly advertised to them. In reality, children are intelligent, discriminating, and skeptical. Despite their lack of experience, they are not that easily fooled.

I don't believe this book could have been written by any of the authors who have published earlier works on children's television. Those authors come at the subject from another view. They are usually pedagogues, advocates, professional critics, or journalists. This is the first book written by a practitioner of children's television for other practitioners.

THE PREVIOUS LITERATURE

The literature about children's television has not been entirely without value to those who work in the medium. On the contrary, some of the books and articles are rich in research detail that has been helpful. Three of the more interesting books are valuable histories spanning the last 25 to 30 years of children's television programs. Gary Grossman's *Saturday Morning TV* is a detailed history of Saturday morning network programs for children. Stuart Fisher's *Kids TV—The First 25 Years* is a statistical reference book. George Woolery's hard-to-find, two-volume *Children's Television: The first 35 years, 1946 - 1981* is an encyclopedic reference book providing the details and credits for every children's show since the inception of the medium. These books, particularly Woolery's scholarly masterpiece, are a joy to the nostalgia and trivia buffs who take a special pleasure in the television of their childhood. These histories are valuable records of a segment of our popular culture. Upon close scrutiny, the flow of children's programs over the past 30 years reveals some important facets of our national ethos.

Apart from these histories, however, most books on children's television have been negatively critical. The books by educators and academics reveal the results of research and studies concerned with the influence of television on children. Journalists have spread the message still further, giving rise to a group of concerned and militant parents, antipathetic to television in general, and agitated particularly by children's television.

Since this body of literature has not been fairly or equally covered by the press and the reviewers, the studies have remained within this core group. Essentially, the writers have been talking to people like themselves—people who would like to see children's television abolished or radically changed. These people cannot make a difference in children's television. The marketers and advertisers of children's products, their advertising and public relations agencies, the people at the three networks, the more than 9,000 new cable systems, and the half-dozen cable programming companies now televising children's fare make the decisions on what children's programs are aired. Writers, artists, and producers of children's programs know little of these books—neither do the syndicators or buyers of children's programs or the growing legions of people tapping movies and television for the licensing of children's products. Worst of all, today's students of journalism, advertising, film arts, communications, and marketing—those who eventually become the new programmers, marketers, and advertisers of children's products as well as the creators of children's shows and commercials for children's products—are not at all familiar with the academic literature on the subject and couldn't care less.

There are some good reasons for the apathy. The people who work in children's television have heard all the arguments about television's harmful effects again and again. The dialog has become tiresome. Is it any wonder that new commentary on the subject is greeted with a "so what else is new" shrug of the shoulders? The arguments and the diatribes don't go anywhere. They don't substantially influence or change the nature of the programs or commercials from year to year.

At best one might say that some of the literature documenting the reactions of children to television, particularly violent material, has heightened the consciousness of a few programmers and creators, though I imagine this has been more from the petitions to the FCC and the resultant accusatory broadsides from advocacy groups at the various hearings in Washington on the subject. Even stone wears away a little with constant pressure.

Perhaps the problem with most of the critical literature about children's television is that it addresses itself to specific problems. And while it points out that the system is faulty, it doesn't deal with changing the system. The people who work within the system aren't interested in changing it either. They simply don't think about it. They know the rules of the game and see little point in playing outside them.

THE PROBLEMS WITH CHILDREN'S TELEVISION

By discussing how to use children's television more effectively, it may seem that I am sweeping all the problems of bad television or too much television under the rug. One can hardly shut out the claims that children's television is a plug-in drug. There are many who advocate doing away with children's television altogether as the best solution. I regard this as an extremist position, but the statistics usually cited by the nay-sayers are clear and alarming. Annually, on average, children between two and eleven years of age watch an average of about 25 hours of television per week all through the year.

The most commonly repeated statistic is that by the time a child graduates from high school today, he or she will have spent more time in front of the television set (17,000 hours) than in a formal classroom (11,000 hours). All the statistics on television viewing from earliest childhood through age eighteen show that no other daily activity, with the exception of sleeping, is so clearly dominant. What's more, the critics have pointed out that most of those hours have been spent watching junk, particularly those shows created for children and aired on the three networks every Saturday morning. One outspoken pundit labeled Saturday morning as a "national tragedy."

Beyond the programming itself, the concern is with the advertising contained in children's programs. It's clear that children are exposed to a large number of commercials. These facts are undeniable, but this is the way it has been for the last 25 years. This is the way advertising is now and, as long as free enterprise exists, the way it will continue to be, despite the barrage of missiles continually fired at all facets of children's television.

Socially, the problem seems to be that we once saw a special vision of human possibility in television and now that vision appears to have been pushed aside for the sake of business. The mistake the educators, critics, and reformers have made is they believe all television is influential, even if it sets out to be entertaining, and that puts a special burden of responsibility on the industry. They are also of the belief that television uses scarce airwaves that belong to the public and consequently, should be in the public interest.

TELEVISION IS FIRST AND FOREMOST A BUSINESS

What these people fail to realize is that commercial television, even for children, is just another business. It is a business that makes its money by helping sell products, a valuable stimulator for gross national product which in turn helps to create jobs and greases the wheels of our economy. Is it fair to ask the television industry to be different from other businesses? Is it fair to ask for more control by the government than other businesses experience?

Those who say television is not in the public interest forget that television is a *mass* medium that sets out to program to the largest possible audience, not a business which custom designs programming to fit every group and individual. It is enough that they design programming for children per se without specific shows for this age group or sex or race or level of intelligence or affluence. The reformers forget that viewers, even child viewers, have choices; they can change the channel; they can turn it off; they can unplug the set and put it in the closet. The reformers overlook the fact that television is very much in the public interest because the public, including children, gets what it wants because programming decisions are based on ratings which accurately tell us what people view in the largest numbers. Many of us make the mistake of wanting the television industry to take more responsibility than we are willing to take ourselves.

Before anyone judges television, he or she must first understand that decisions in the television industry are economic decisions.

The television business works on three simple principles: keep the audience up, the costs down, and the regulators out. The reformers forget that television's first mission is not to inform, educate, or enlighten. It isn't even to entertain. Its first mission is to entice viewers to watch the commercials. If commercial television cannot move goods, it cannot be in business. Just because commercial television devotes many of its hours to the special audience of children doesn't change the fundamental point of view one iota.

The commercial networks and stations are willing to program a certain amount of their schedules for children. That is, they are willing if someone will pay for it. That revenue contributes a good portion of their profits. Since the children's market is a substantial one, a considerable body of advertisers invest hundreds of millions of dollars each year to tell almost 45 million children about their products.

THE CHILDREN'S MARKET

Accounting for one-fifth of the U.S. population, 44.3 million kids under 12 comprise the children's market: 22.7 million boys, 21.6 million girls. Thirty-six million of them are white, 6.7 million are blacks, and 1.6 million are of other races.

Almost one-third of the children under 12 live with only one parent, 87 percent of whom live with their mothers. According to the Bureau of Labor Statistics, 23 million of today's children are growing up in dual-income families. Day-care centers are busier than ever. One survey indicates that more than 5 million families have their children in the care of day-care professionals.

The Bureau of Census reports a short-lived but significant growth in the children's market. A two percent rise in births brought 3.7 million kids into the market in 1984. The Bureau expects the under-five population to swell to more than 19 million by 1990, then shrink back to 17.6 million in 2000 and up to 17.7 million in 2050.

Technically speaking, a child is not much of a consumer. Disposable income means spare change from his or her parents. Weekly allowances have increased in the past two years. The going rate is $2.50 for 10-year olds, $3.00 for 11-year olds, and $5.00 for 12-year olds. Ninety percent of this disposable income is disposed of quickly in candy, department, and toy stores. Kids are highly skilled, however, at getting their parents to purchase what they can't buy for themselves. In this sense they represent considerable consumer buying power.

Kids' activities have not changed dramatically in recent years except that 82 percent of elementary schools now use computers in the classroom. While children no longer walk to the movie theater every Saturday afternoon for a matinee, most still see an average of six movies a year. Eighteen and one-third million kids see at least one movie per year. Organized sports continue to play a big part in children's lives. About 3.5 million participate in YMCA or other sports leagues. Every year 2.5 million boys, aged 10-12 play little league basketball, and soccer is becoming an important new sport.

Television is, of course, a major activity. Eighty-five million American families own at least one television set—91 percent of them in color. Forty-nine million own more than one set. More than half of the 85 million television households get cable.

According to a recent Nielsen report, two-to-five year olds watch, on average, about 28.5 hours per week, about an hour and a half more than they did ten years ago. About 25 percent of that is daytime weekday watching. Fourteen percent of the prime time audience between 8:00 P.M. and 9:00 P.M. (E.S.T.) are children under 12. For two to three hours every Saturday morning, children crowd in front of the television set. A hit prime-time network show might draw as many as 9 million child viewers, while the average weekend cartoons get 4.3 million.

While there are more than 84 million home radios—one in virtually every home—no one seems to know how many kids listen to what. Pulse, Inc., once an authority on kid's listening habits, stopped studying kids more than 15 years ago. Except for a small and fledgling Children's Radio Network, there isn't a children's program left on commercial radio.

As for print media, children have not picked up their parent's newspaper and magazine reading habits. A survey by the National Assessment of Educational Progress indicated that children read "for only short periods of time. About 41 percent of 13-year olds say they glean some news from a newspaper every day, while 23 percent said they get some news from magazines every week." When the choices for free time activity are television, movies, a book, or a magazine, only two percent of five-year olds and four percent of 13-year olds surveyed opted to pick up a magazine.

Overwhelmingly, television is far and away practically the only medium to reach this market consistently and in large numbers.

THE CHILDREN'S ADVERTISERS

There are more than 75 corporations in the United States that make goods or provide services for children on a national basis. Some of these companies are household names: General Foods, General Mills, Kelloggs, Quaker, and Ralston; Coleco, Hasbro, and Mattel; Hershey's, Mars M&Ms, and Nabisco Brands; American Greetings and Hallmark; Walt Disney, Hanna-Barbera, and Warner Communications; Burger King and McDonalds.

Besides these familiar companies, there are a great many more who provide goods or services in a variety of categories. The products they make and distribute are toys, candy, cereals, ice cream, carbonated and non-carbonated soft drinks, chewing gum, snacks, baked goods, fast foods, pasta products, lunch meats, clothing and shoes, motion pictures, video games, phonograph records, books, and bicycles. On a local level, there are the retailers who specialize in these goods, not to speak of services like amusement parks and ice cream stores that are frequented by children, teens, and young families. These companies invest more than $500 million per year in advertising, most of it in television because it is the most efficient and effective way of communicating with children who influence the purchases of these goods and services.

These are the companies who pay the bills for children's television. I daresay, without them, commercial children's television would not exist.

THE PROBLEM OF ENTERTAINING CHILDREN

To attract their fair share of the advertising expenditures from these companies, commercial networks and stations program material they believe will attract the largest number of children. In most cases these programs tend to be cartoon entertainment or comedies because they are the kinds of shows most children like and are shown at times when children control the television dial. These are the shows to which they will most likely turn. These are also the shows critics maintain have turned television into a junkyard. These are the shows that many parents deplore and complain about—they can't understand why television isn't providing their children with something better.

The fact is that better shows, programs with more substance, have been tried over and over again by the commercial networks and stations. For the most part they have not attracted a large audience and consequently are not economically practical. There is only so much of this kind of programming that television is willing to support.

Deeper issues go beyond the concerns that our children are spending too much of their time watching tasteless and insensitive junk. There is deep concern about the perpetuation of violent behavior. A body of research suggests children imitate what they see on television, that the violent stories they watch leave a permanent imprint on their characters and personalities.

While some people would have you believe this is a new phenomena created by television, this is actually an ancient question.

> Don't you understand, I replied, that we begin by telling children stories, which taken as a whole, are fiction, though they contain some truth? Such story telling begins at an earlier age than physical training; that is why I said we should start with the mind. And the beginning, as you know, is always the most

important part, when the character is being molded and easily takes an impression one may wish to stamp on it. Then shall we simply allow our children to listen to any stories that anyone happens to make up, and so receive into their minds ideas often the very opposite of those we shall think they ought to have when they grow up?

(PLATO, The Republic)

The world's thinkers, even in ancient Greece, have always been wary of those who wish to entertain children. And well they should be. The solution to the television problem is the same one that has served for all media through time. Parents must take the responsibility of scrutinizing, understanding, and monitoring the media served to their children.

IS ADVERTISING TO CHILDREN UNFAIR?

Another philosophical (and practical) concern with children's television focuses on the commercials. Parents and critics complain that advertising to children is inherently unfair. They are made to want things they don't need; the nagging for things advertised on television creates disruption in the family; that advertising to children is like shooting fish in a barrel. The extremists who hold these views believe all advertising to children should be abolished, and indeed, they have strongly urged the government on many occasions to consider this alternative, fully recognizing that it may mean abolishing television for children altogether.

While I believe we have occasionally presented too many unclear, even dishonest advertising messages to children in too short a time, entirely eliminating advertising to children doesn't make any sense. Without advertising, children's television cannot exist.

Advertising is part of a child's socialization process in our culture and protecting him from it does no good in the end. As with all products, as long as companies make things for children, they will find ways to advertise them.

What these advertising critics fail to understand is that all products for children do not succeed just because they are advertised. If they did, then one must explain why the overwhelming percentage of new products fail each year. One must explain why a controversial children's product like the Barbie doll has been selling successfully for more than 25 years, while its countless imitators like Dusty, Chrissy, and Dawn haven't lasted more than a year or so. One must explain why there hasn't been a successful new candy bar in years despite frequent attempts by major companies. Even a candy bar with Reggie Jackson's name on it at the peak of his baseball career couldn't be put across on television or the candy counters. One must explain why the country's largest and most successful marketer, Procter & Gamble, hasn't successfully launched "Pringles," a new potato chip, a product of which children are the major consumer. One must explain why certain breakfast cereals have been around since radio days, successful then and successful now, while numerous others have tried and failed. One can argue about television's ability to get someone to try something once, but one must then explain the reorder.

If parents had a clearer understanding of how and why many children's products came into their home, they might become more aware of their selections, even more judicious. They would realize they can allow the medium of television to shape their lives or they can actively resist it— but they would also stop having unrealistic expectations from it.

Whether you are a professional communicator, a parent, or both, I hope you will not conclude that I am putting up a spirited defense of television or that I'm trying to convince you that its problems are inconsequential.

Just because television is first and foremost a business doesn't mean you should stop squirming with discomfort when you see tasteless junk. Nor am I advocating you relax into the ether of futility and surrender either your principles or the nation's children to pragmatism. I am merely pointing out that there are a considerable number of positive aspects to children's television, and I, for one, think it is worth saving. Because complaining about television, jumping on it, kicking it, or trying to beat it to death hasn't helped much in the last 25 years, I am suggesting another way. Make it better by making it more interesting. Know the audience better and respect the audience more, and you can use the language of television with children more skillfully. Learn the limitations of what you can say or show clearly and you will be accused less of dishonesty or chicanery. After all, understanding something is the first step toward handling it.

By clearly understanding how children's television works, you may come away feeling that children's television isn't as bad as all that, at least not as bad as some would like you to think. Perhaps the criticism leveled at children's television is better focused on our whole economic system since television itself is simply an outgrowth of the free marketplace. Perhaps, by understanding it better, you will come to believe that children's television is an important reflection of American popular culture and is no more harmful than the comics, comic books, and radio programs that preceded it and are now looked upon wistfully as having been some of the most wonderful experiences of our youth.

By revealing an insider's view and an attitude more sympathetic to television, I hope I will capture the attention of professional communicators and students more fully than the critical literature preceding it.

It is my hope to provide the less experienced with a fuller understanding of children's television that can be used every day by people who want to touch the hearts and minds of children.

Overall, I think there are benefits for any audience in understanding children better, and consequently serving them better as people whose needs are separate and special. While it may be too much to hope for, I'd like to see an end to the controversy and stress. I'd like to see better children's products and services; I'd like to see both products, services and television, provide genuine need fulfillment; I'd like to see more honest communication with children in advertising; I'd like to see increased creativity, sensitivity, and imagination in children's progams; and I'd like to see children respected for the potential they represent as people and not simply for the potential they represent as consumers of goods and services.

This is a guide book for the people who can make that difference—not by dissent, but by practicing their business, art, and craft in more effective ways with this special audience.

It is my hope that the collected experience conveyed in this book will help you do that.

CHAPTER 2

1955: The Electronic Pied Piper Comes of Age

THE MODERN ERA OF CHILDREN'S TELEVISION BEGAN IN 1955. SOME BROADCAST historians might date it earlier by a few years, but I mark it at the advent of Walt Disney's "Mickey Mouse Club" in early November 1955. This was the first network show that aired one hour a day, five days a week, at a time when most children were home and in control of the television set. No other show before it reached as many children with as much frequency. And no other show before it was used as effectively by advertisers of children's products. CBS also introduced "Captain Kangaroo" to television in 1955. Never enormously popular in terms of high ratings, this gentle little show for preschool children featuring Bob Keeshan as the lovable Captain Kangaroo, holds the distinction of being the longest running kids show on television. The show is no longer on CBS, and is now playing on public television.

CHILDREN'S TELEVISION: 1947 TO 1955

Unquestionably, children's television existed before 1955. Some even call the early years a golden age in children's television because they remember the shows as being so entertaining and wholesome in comparison with today's fare.

Permanent records of those shows exist only as the scratchiest kinescopes, making them difficult to compare with today's programs, so I daresay that most of the comparisons exist in people's memories of a quieter, more gracious time.

I do not mean to disparage the production quality of those early television shows at all. Some of them were truly wonderful. Played at first in the early evening at 7:00 P.M. and 7:30 P.M. (E.S.T.) and later on Saturday mornings, there probably never were bigger favorites than "Howdy Doody," the first television show for kids, and "Kukla, Fran and Ollie," which followed shortly thereafter.

In their earliest years, these shows played in the evening because the networks were trying to sell television sets and it was important to demonstrate how television brought the family together and had something for everyone, even the kids.

The morning, Saturday, and weekday shows were much tamer then and were certainly far more enlightening than today's fare. Shows such as "Mr. Wizard" and "Mr. I-magination" were early attempts to make information entertaining for kids. Don Herbert, who played "Mr. Wizard" on NBC in the late '40s and early '50s, was always one of my favorites; when I managed Nickelodeon, the cable network for children, I brought him back to television in an updated version of his show. His ratings today are still among the best on the Nickelodeon network.

"Ding Dong School," with Miss Frances, was a delight for preschoolers and this show's format was one of the first, along with "Romper Room," to be copied all over the world by broadcasters in every language.

The Saturday morning cartoon day part as we know it today did not exist. Saturday mornings brought forth sporadic, occasional shows, but the networks did not play two- or three-hour blocks of children's shows as they do today. The networks had not yet realized the value in a children's market, beyond making them an influential force in a family's decision to buy a television set. The economic incentive of massive children's advertising did not yet exist.

Children's shows appeared to be better supported on a local rather than a national level. Most local television shows for children were combinations of live television and film shorts made for the theatrical market. Most shows had a host—a Sheriff John, an Engineer Bill, or a Space Captain who entertained children at the station each day and played old Popeye cartoons, which in those days were enormously popular.

Occasionally, a local market would develop something more original. In Los Angeles, for example, a young comedian named Stan Freberg did a live show called "Beany and Cecil." Stan did most of the puppeteering and some of the voices along with another very talented fellow named Dawes Butler, who went on to become the voice of Huckelberry Hound as well as many other famous animated characters. Freberg, of course, later gained national fame as a smash hit recording artist and a practitioner of funny commercials. "Beany and Cecil" was eventually developed into an animated show by Bob Clampett, the creator and producer of the original show.

Few production companies or broadcasters invested any substantial money in creating new television fare for children. There simply weren't enough advertisers asking for it, and without the demand, programmers were satisfied to run live shows produced at the local stations or play old Popeye cartoons and Hopalong Cassidy movies. Even the cereal industry, which traditionally advertised to children on the radio, moved very slowly into television. Total advertising expenditures for the cereal industry in 1956 were about $25 million, in contrast to $460 million today. ($150 million is spent on children's advertising.) Toy advertising was virtually non-existent.

The mid-1950s produced an ideal environment for children's programming and advertising to blossom. The economic climate was good. The nation was still rebuilding as part of the postwar program. Veterans returning from World War II were starting families in what would later be called the Baby Boom. With the Depression years long past, these years embraced prosperity, new technology, new products, and new marketing techniques.

America had begun its love affair with television. Sets were now available at affordable prices and television had proven itself our most important medium.

The children of these times were brought into the world by parents who grew up during the Depression and spent their young adult years fighting a war. Now that they were settled down and living peaceful, prosperous lives, they wanted more for their children than they had experienced themselves. They wanted backyards with pools, good schools, new bikes, stylish clothes, plenty of new and nutritional foods, and entertainment of every kind. It was a permissive era. The child became king. The time was ripe for television to direct itself to children's interests and wants.

Over the next 15 to 20 years, television for children became what it is today. New production techniques were developed, traditional time slots were set, advertising to children became big business, and the licensing business took on new muscle, becoming an industry unto itself. Virtually all the innovations—the development of new marketing and advertising techniques, and the important research on children as an audience—took place during these years. What appears to be a new development today is merely a rehash and dressing up of an idea originally formulated years ago.

A Handful of Pioneers

For the practitioner in children's television today, it is important to study the history and development in these years because they reveal the key principles of children's programming and advertising, the marketing techniques that were successful, and those that failed. The pitfalls and the lessons to be learned are gained from studying the activities of a few companies that made the industry successful through trial and error: the three networks and other major market stations, Disney and Hanna-Barbera in original production, Warner's and MGM in syndication and licensing, Kelloggs and General Mills in cereals, General Foods in non-carbonated drinks, Mattel in toys, and Mars M&M's in the candy business. These, for the most part, are the companies that pioneered the children's television business as we know it today and set the patterns and principles for the years to come.

I entered children's television in 1953. Having graduated from the University of Southern California School of Journalism and having taken a Master's degree at New York University, I returned to California to begin work in a tiny advertising agency named Carson/Roberts. We had six people and a handful of small accounts. I started in February 1953 as a trainee, first learning the business and after a few months becoming what was then known as a copy-contact man.

Mattel: The Company That Changed the Toy Industry

In November 1954, Carson/Roberts went to work for a tiny little toy company, Mattel Creations, in Hawthorne, California. Their annual sales at the time were approximately $4 million and their annual advertising budget approximately $150,000—a fairly good-sized account for a small agency in those days.

Only a few years before, Elliot and Ruth Handler, a young couple from Denver, started their company in a garage. (Curiously enough, Elliot had come to California to work at Disney and spent a short time there as a designer.) Elliot cut out and glued plastic doll furniture from old picture frame remnants and Ruth sold it. In these early years the Handlers took on a partner named Harold Mattson. Harold's last name and Elliot's first were combined to form a name for the company. Mattson held a patent for an extruded rubber belt, which, when turned, could pluck a metal comb and produce a song. This device was placed inside of musical toys—a Jack-in-the-Box, a piano, a guitar. Mattel's first products were colorful low price adaptations of the old Swiss music box. The Handlers eventually bought the patent rights from Mattson and moved from the garage to a made-over Chinese laundry and ultimately to a small factory in Hawthorne, a suburb of South Los Angeles. By the time we met, the company had a small reputation in the toy industry as a maker of musical toys, primarily a Jack-in-the-Box that played "Pop Goes the Weasel."

In 1954 the sales volume of the toy industry was less than $1 billion (as opposed to more than $12 billion today). The leading company was Marx Toys with $50 million in sales per year. Advertising toys was virtually unknown. The entire toy industry invested less than $1 million per year in advertising. (Today, the amount exceeds $300 million.) In December 1955, Louis Marx, the founder and owner of Marx Toys, appeared on the cover of *Time* magazine, the only time anyone from the toy industry has been so honored. The cover story featured Marx but also provided coverage on other important toy companies. Mattel wasn't even mentioned. In the same story, Louis Marx boasted that he had spent only $312.00 in advertising the previous year. He maintained that advertising did not and could not sell toys.

Ralph Carson, the founder of Carson/Roberts and the man who hired me, managed the Mattel toy account personally but assigned me the day-to-day contact, the planning of details, and whatever copy work needed to be done.

I started learning the toy business and was planning Mattel's meager $150,000 budget. Most of the budget was allocated to fundamentals—a catalog for their customers and some trade advertising. We reserved $60,000 to invest in some local children's television shows in major markets just before Christmas.

In those years, a few toy companies used local television programs and their commercials were usually presented by the local host, Sheriff John, Engineer Bill, or an equivalent. These performers usually demonstrated the toy in front of a live audience and whatever efficacy was lost in demonstration was made up in mock enthusiasm and seconds beyond the allotted 60. This was recognized as an exceedingly limited use of television, reaching only very young children in major markets. At best, it was an experimental shot in the dark. No one we knew could point to any concrete success with this technique, but we believed it was probably the best use of limited funds. At least the technique allowed us to talk to children, the ultimate consumer, rather than to moms whom the toy industry regarded as the only family member to influence. We did not share this prevailing opinion.

There was one short-lived try at *national* television toy advertising on a show called "Toyorama" which ran a few weeks before Christmas on Saturday morning network television. The show was really designed to tell about upcoming Christmas toys and to be informative rather than entertaining. Few toy makers cared enough to sponsor the show and it was never taken seriously by the industry.

Enter "The Mickey Mouse Club"

As our plans for Christmas 1955 were developing, a west coast sales representative from the ABC television network called the agency. His name was Vince Francis, a dapper and charming French-Italian from San Francisco. (That ABC—West Coast operated out of San Francisco in those days says something significant about Los Angeles' relative lack of importance as an advertising center in the '50s.) At our first meeting none of us even dreamt that Vince would become, over the next 10 years, one of our closest business associates.

Vince came to tell us about a new development at ABC. The courageous little network had made arrangements with Walt Disney's studio to program a new Disney-created children's show. It was to air an hour a day, five days a week, starting at 5:00 P.M. each afternoon. Normally this time period was station option time for ABC's network affiliates. They played their own local shows rather than taking a feed from the network. The Walt Disney name was so powerful that the network believed the vast majority of their affiliates would give up their own time and carry the Disney show in it. ABC was so confident they were guaranteeing 90 percent coverage of all the television homes in the country. The show was to be called "The Mickey Mouse Club" and ABC promised it would reach almost every child in America on a daily basis.

Nothing like it had been tried since the early days of television with "Kukla, Fran and Ollie" and the "Howdy Doody Show." Besides that, it was the first time the Disney theatrical cartoon library would be shown on television. Mickey Mouse had been an international movie favorite since the late '20s and Mickey was to star in the new series. The show was to combine music, songs, cartoons, children's news features, adventure serials, and appearances by guest celebrities along with a supporting cast of young performers called Mouseketeers.

At the time, this was the most ambitious piece of entertainment ever mounted for children and the expense to Disney and to ABC was enormous. They needed unprecedented advertising support to make the venture successful.

There was little question in our minds that the show would be a hit with the television audience, but the price of sponsorships, unfortunately, was prohibitive for a tiny company like Mattel. Sponsorship was sold on a 52-week, non-cancellable basis. Five hundred thousand dollars per year gave a sponsor a quarter-hour, once a week segment in which three commercials were shown. ABC needed 20 such sponsors to fill the available commercial time.

The half-million dollar price tag was simply out of reach for a small toy company, and the use of 52 weeks a year of advertising went in direct opposition to the toy industry's yearly sales pattern in which 80 percent of the sales were made in the last three months of the year. Few people thought about buying toys at other than the pre-Christmas period.

Normally, most advertising agencies weighing a situation such as this one would have dismissed the proposition at the outset. They may have recognized the opportunity but then reasoned it was too rich for a small client. Frankly, we felt that way. Yet, since this was a major television development for children and sure to set new trends, we felt obliged to at least inform the Handlers about the forthcoming show and tell them what this opportunity might mean to one of the larger companies in their industry.

In 1955 there were no recognized brand names in toys. Household names such as Mattel, Hasbro, and Fisher-Price were unknown to the consumer. An adult buying a toy for a child went into a conventional toy store and asked for something appropriate for a six year old girl or a nine year old boy or perhaps the fad product of the particular season if there were one. (Imagine doing that today at a Toys-R-Us.) Since children had limited exposure to specific toys, even they hardly knew what to ask for. Adults bought the toy they thought suitable and hoped the child would enjoy it. It is also important to remember that these were also the years when young men and women, brought up in the Depression, had survived a war and were starting to raise families. These young Depression-reared parents wanted much more for their children than they had in their own childhoods.

It seemed apparent to us that with this new blockbuster television show promising to reach all the children in the country, there was an opportunity to build the first brand name in toys. We believed the child who would say "That's what I want, Daddy" was going to be an extremely persuasive salesman.

Both Ralph Carson and Jack Roberts felt a close personal connection to this situation since they had just returned from the war and were starting their own families. The Handlers were starting a family as well and quickly understood what we were saying about the condition of the times and the opportunity that was waiting. In addition, Elliot Handler, who had worked at Disney, was thoroughly taken with Disney's magical touch with youngsters. He was also convinced that no one could reach children as well.

The price however, staggered all of us. Although we had faith in the show's ability to attract a large children's audience, none of us were completely convinced that advertising toys to children could dramatically increase toy sales. It simply hadn't been tried on a meaningful scale. We were surprised at first that the Handlers even considered the proposition so seriously. We were later to learn more about the gambling instincts of this remarkable young couple.

The Handlers called in their comptroller and explained the proposition. Essentially, they wanted to know what would happen to their company if they gambled $500,000 on advertising and it didn't work. The comptroller pointed out that the entire net worth of the company was then $500,000 and that sum represented all the money the Handler's had. Losing the $500,000 might not bankrupt the company, but it would leave them badly bent out of shape and with a shakey credit record. Without much further deliberation the Handlers decided to go ahead with the sponsorship of "The Mickey Mouse Club." They commissioned us to draw up the contract, proceed with the plans for advertising, and develop two television commercials to run on the show that fall.

THE SHOTS HEARD ROUND THE WORLD

The first two Mattel commercials were devoted to Jack-in-the-Boxes and Getars, the musical toy line. Another commercial advertised a new product, The Burp Gun. The Burp Gun was an automatic cap-firing machine gun modeled after the machine guns used in WWII jungle fighting. Instead of playing war with it on television, we showed young Cary Carson

1. ANNCR: (VO) One day, a few
    weeks ago, I looked all over the
    house for Billy.

2. Of course, I found out later
    that my son was in darkest
    Africa.

3. Billy was hunting elephants
    with his trusty Mattel Toy
    Burp Gun.

4. That's the only fully automatic
    cap gun in the world, you
    know.

5. Real safe. Fires one shot,
    (SFX: SHOTS)

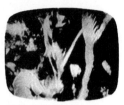

6. (SFX: ELEPHANTS) or in
    bursts. He never misses with
    that Burp Gun.

7. (SFX: SHOTS/ELEPHANTS)

8. And it's so simple to play with.
    The safety catch keeps it from
    firing while Billy winds it,

9. then he closes the breech and
    checks his ammunition.

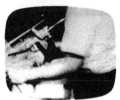

10. There's plenty of room for
    spare caps in the magazine.

11. He's off again. Hunting tigers
    in India.

12. But don't worry, the Burp Gun
    is so safe,

13. it's got the Parents Seal Of
    Approval. Only $4 wherever
    toys are sold.

14. (SFX: SHOTS) You can tell

15. it's Mattel. It's swell.

> *Mattel's Burp Gun was the first toy commercial ever put on film. It aired on "The Mickey Mouse Club" in November 1955. It was the first televised toy that became an immediate hit. (Courtesy, Mattel, Inc.)*

(Ralph Carson's son) stalking a herd of wild elephants in his living room. With rearscreen projection the elephants appeared and retreated with the film in reverse whenever Cary got off a burst. Jack Roberts and I wrote and directed these commercials and produced them at the staggering price of $2,500 each.

There was something added to these commercials which became a model for other children's advertisers. Jack Roberts developed a new logo for Mattel, taking their existing capital M with a boy and a crown leaning against it and encapsulated the M inside of a cerrated red seal. The boy with the crown was also placed seated in the crotch of the M. Jack's reasoning was that younger children who could not read letter forms would recognize a cerrated seal shape. When the logo was used on television, it was reinforced with a catchy slogan, "You can tell it's Mattel . . . it's swell." It was intended as a mnemonic visual device to get kids to remember the logo and the Mattel name.

This idea was much copied later by other toy companies and other television advertisers for kids. It's a concept that worked in 1955 and is working for others today.

Walt Disney's "Mickey Mouse Club" made its debut on television in November 1955. As predicted, the show was an immediate hit. The ratings swamped everything in that time slot. Other stations would not even program anything very strong against it. From 5:00 P.M. to 6:00 P.M. on weekdays, the show dominated the airwaves, and every Wednesday from 5:30 to 5:45 when Mattel played their three commercials, 90 percent of the nation's kids were watching the first toy commercials ever put on film.

The big shock, however, was that by Thanksgiving we had not yet felt an impact from the advertising. Mattel had shipped their merchandise to the wholesalers, who in turn had sold it in and stocked the retail shelves. All was ready and waiting. Except the phones were quiet. We left for the long Thanksgiving weekend feeling glum, anxious, and worried. We were even considering rushing out and placing full-page newspaper ads in major markets to remind parents of our television advertising. It was a backup plan, a desperation move. We started to believe the gamble had failed.

Monday brought a new perspective. When we returned to work after the Thanksgiving weekend, the phones were ringing off the hook. The Mattel people literally could not get into the front door of their factory because of the piled up sacks of mail—all orders. The lesson we learned, and it has not changed since, was that the long chain of distribution then predominant in the toy industry had simply taken its time to produce results that could be felt at the factory. From sales representative to toy wholesaler (jobber) sales force to retail store was an uncommonly awkward process and it simply took four to six weeks before the advertiser could feel the impact at retail. Reorders were the only tangible evidence that the advertised products were selling.

This same distribution system exists in the toy industry today, except now there are sales measuring services in the field who issue computerized reports to their subscribers.

Before Christmas 1955, Mattel had shipped more than one million Burp Guns at $4.00 each. Considering the company's previous annual sales volume for their entire line of products was only $4 million, this was unheard of success. They had more than doubled their sales volume. The demand for the Burp Gun was so great, there wasn't even a part to be found in the stores. Herb Caen, the famous columnist from San Francisco, called us with a special request to find him a Burp Gun; we even received a letter from President Eisenhower asking us to find a Burp Gun for his grandson David. The Burp Gun had fired shots heard round the world. The world's toy industry stood up and took notice, but strangely enough regarded this first entrance into television advertising as a fluke. Instead of copying, competitors decided to watch and wait.

The following February Mattel went to the annual New York Toy Fair with signs in their showroom saying "Remember the Burp Gun." Buyers wrote orders right off the reel of television commercials and the schedule of when they would run. Overnight, a skeptical and doubting trade, including the larger scale wholesalers who dominated the industry and literally dictated terms to the manufacturers, fell under the spell of television. They stopped evaluating Mattel toys by their individual charm and sales appeal. The product's television budget and schedule were almost more important.

THE NEW TOYS ON TELEVISION

The people at Mattel and the agency, flushed with success on television, began thinking of toys in an entirely different way. We began to see toys as concepts that could be depicted or demonstrated in television commercials. Prior to television, the industry stayed away from complicated or conceptual products that did not read right off the shelf. Some manufacturers hired demonstrators to demonstrate a complicated product in department stores at Christmas. This was an expensive and limited technique, to say the least. Television allowed us to break away from that kind of restricted thinking. Presenting the product on television became part of the product. We realized early on that, for children, the product as seen in a television commercial *was* the product.

In showing our earliest television commercials to children, we also realized something more important that persists to this day. The play situation in which you place a toy becomes a fantasy for the child. The fantasy presented becomes as important as the product.

The Western Fantasy

Mattel, responding to the craze for Westerns on television in the late '50s, decided to bring out an authentic line of Western guns and holsters. The cap pistols looked like real bone-handled .45 six shooters and the holsters and gun belts were genuine leather.

Because little boys watching Westerns were familiar with such gun-slinging techniques as fast draws and fanning multiple shots from a single-action revolver, the new Mattel cap pistols came with a fanning feature. No kid had been able to do that with a cap pistol before. We called this toy gun the Fanner 50.

In writing those commercials, I chose not to imitate the new television Westerns. To achieve a simpler, more exaggerated Western fantasy, I returned to my memories of Saturday matinee serials with Buck Jones and Ken Maynard, to the Tom Mix movies and radio programs, and to the Lone Ranger and Tonto. What I remembered and liked best was how slick those old cowboys handled their guns. I studied Western six-shooter lore and learned about fast draws and gun tricks which involved spinning the guns in and out of a holster. I also learned that those tricks had such colorful names in the Old West as "The Curly Bill" or "The Road Agent's Spin." I learned them myself and they were fun.

I wrote those tricks into our demonstration of the Fanner 50 on television. I convinced Mattel to include a little comic book with each product so that kids could learn the tricks. For our commercial, we cast a boy whose father was a movie cowboy and who had already learned some of those fancy gun tricks from his Dad. The boy, Matty, became the hero in our television commercials. He demonstrated the guns in familiar good guys versus bad guys, Western fantasy situations. Fanner 50s became, with young boys, more than just a cap pistol to point and shoot, Fanner 50s became toys you could do as many tricks with as you could with a Yo-Yo.

Demonstrating those tricks and expanding the limitations of playing with a cap pistol into a boy's cowboy fantasy could not have been achieved without television.

This line of Western products, along with a line of licensed Mickey Mouse Club toys, became the Mattel hits in their first few years in television. Sales in successive years increased from $4 million to $9 million to $13 million, then $18 million. When the nation's children grew tired of "The Mickey Mouse Club," we developed our own half-hour network show on ABC called "Matty's Funday Funnies." This show was essentially a library of such old Harvey theatrical cartoons as "Baby Hughey" and "Casper the Friendly Ghost" welded together in wrap arounds with two other original animated characters we developed, "Matty Mattel and Sister Belle." The show played regularly on Sundays at 5:00 P.M., so we created a song and titles with a lyric that changed Sunday to Funday.

THE MOST POPULAR TOY IN HISTORY: THE BARBIE STORY

By 1958 Mattel had become the industry leader in musical toys and toy guns. They clearly needed a girl's product to balance the boy's action category The need prompted the introduction of the Barbie doll. In the years since, the fantastic success of this product has become part of our popular culture. Barbie became, far and away, the most popular toy product in history.

For almost 30 years she has been a best seller. Barbie products have sold more than $1 billion at retail since their inception and the names "Barbie" and "Ken" have come into our language with much wider meanings than names for dolls. Is there anyone in America over the age of three who doesn't know about Barbie?

More than any other children's product before or since, the Barbie doll is testimony to the influence of television advertising on children. The Barbie phenomenon cannot be regarded as just another popular children's product or even just an effective television advertising campaign for children. The Barbie doll, its essential appeal, how it is positioned, how it affects children, and why it has lasted so long is a significant social commentary on the television age. There is no better example to illustrate many of the points I've tried to make in this book. If one is truly interested in how post '50s television has functioned as an electronic pied piper with children, then the Barbie doll must command very special attention.

Which one is the Barbie doll? The two on the left are Lili dolls made in Germany from which the Barbie doll was modeled. Mattel bought the rights to Lili before they brought out the original Barbie doll, on the right. This 1959 first-run brunette, in "mint, in the box" condition sells for up to $1,750. Blonds are slightly cheaper. (Courtesy, Paul Guggenheim, left; courtesy, Mattel, Inc., right)

One must realize that when Barbie was introduced she was truly a strange looking doll. It didn't seem to matter that she had a bitchy look, with pouted lips and an icy stare. Girls didn't seem to mind her awkward stiff legs with their high-heeled arch. And few commented that her rather ample breasts had no nipple. Somehow Barbie filled a very special need for little girls' imaginations. She was the fulfillment of every little girl's dream of glamor, fame, wealth, and stardom.

There are all manner of stories and myths about how Barbie originated. Major stories about Barbie and her origins were published in *Life, Look,* and *The Saturday Evening Post.* Art Buchwald wrote numerous columns about her. The media coverage of Barbie in the past 25 years has been staggering.

Curiously enough, however, I have yet to see anything in print which has reported the story accurately. The Barbie doll did not spring from the mind of a Mattel inventor. Nor did the idea of an 11½" inch doll with breasts come from Ruth Handler's imagination as some stories have told it. Barbie had a progenitor and her name was Lili.

Lili was a German doll modeled after a German playgirl in cartoon form who regularly graced the pages of *Das Bild,* a German newspaper much like our *Inquirer.* The Lili doll was not designed to appeal to children, but was sold to adult men in tobacconists and bars. Lili came in one of two sexy outfits, and if there was an aura or fantasy at all around this doll, it was as an adult male's pet.

The doll was hardly known in the United States and Paul Guggenheim, a Swiss who originally distributed Lili in the United States, remembers he was only able to sell a few of the dolls to Uncle Bernie's, an expensive toy import shop in Beverly Hills.

When the Handlers first saw this doll they were intrigued with the possibilities of a three-dimensional mannequin. Ruth Handler's daughter Barbara was playing with paper dolls at the time and Ruth recognized how much more fun paper dolls might be if there were a doll or a mannequin who could wear real miniature garments made of fabric with actual buttons and zippers.

An emissary was sent to Germany and all the rights to Lili were bought by Mattel. Some doll construction patents were bought from Hauser, the German manufacturer, and the cartoon rights to Lili were bought and put aside.

Although Elliot Handler was usually adamant against widely testing a highly classified toy project, the concept of bringing out this type of product in the United States was considered so radical that Elliot was persuaded to test this new doll with a few hundred mothers and their children. The test results were astoundingly clear cut. Almost 100 percent of the mothers literally hated the doll and felt it was too mature for their little girls. Most said they would never buy it. Almost 100 percent of the girls, shown the doll independent of their mothers, said they loved the doll and definitely wanted to own it.

Based on the children's reactions and the Handler's new-found faith in television's ability to communicate a story to children, the Handlers decided to proceed. The Lili doll was renamed after Barbara Handler and Barbie was born.

60 SECONDS

1. (MUSIC UNDER) ANNCR: (VO) This is the year of the Barbie Look

2. and the Barbie Look is the fashion look.

3. That's right. Correct. The swinginest, liveliest, zinginest fashions

4. of the Barbie Look.

5. Come feast your eyes on Barbie and Midge and look at the Barbie Look.

6. The hairdo's the big news.

7. The fashions are smashin'. For night or day; for school or play,

8. the look is the Barbie Look.

9. Look what's happened to Ken and Allen, his friend with new bendable legs. They're really the end.

10. So like Midge and Barbie, they're better by far, because they all have the look. The fashion look.

11. The great new Barbie Look.

12. There's one, and two, and three, and four, and that's only the beginning, there's a whole lot more.

13. So get on down to see the Barbie Look in the fashions and the dolls as well.

14. You're gonna love 'em all

15. because after all, you can tell they're Mattel. They're swell. (MUSIC OUT)

The Barbie doll was treated as a fashion icon in her early television commercials. The "Barbie Look" became little girls' idea of a "fashion look." (Courtesy, Mattel, Inc.)

The actual manufacturing of Barbie was another Mattel innovation. Mattel had been conducting some experiments with cottage industries in Japan and had determined that a quality product could be made there in this manner. Mattel set up numerous small factories to do the blow-molding of the doll itself, but the costumes were made by thousands of laborers cutting and sewing at home. Barbie was one of the first quality products to come out of post-war Japan.

Mattel assigned the task of positioning the doll, the logo, and the package design, as well as introducing the doll on television to Carson/Roberts. We immediately recognized the doll as one that presented a new play situation for girls, in effect, a new fantasy. Watching children play with the doll, we concluded that little girls saw Barbie as the young woman they wanted to be someday. All the previous dolls were babies they could mother in the play situation. The Barbie doll gave growing girls an opportunity to make a short fantasy leap to becoming a teenager and wearing pretty clothes. This factor was the key in the doll's appeal.

In our first television commercials and for many years thereafter we didn't depict Barbie as a doll. We treated her like a real-life teenage fashion model. This was an early example of the product positioned as a personality. Each 60-second commercial was a story in the life of Barbie and the events of the story provided reasons for her to change into her many costumes.

Her fashion poses were photographed in front of stylized realistic backgrounds, first paper sculpture and then more realistic settings. Children seeing her on television accepted her as a real person.

Because Barbie was presented as a teenage model, we took great pains to make her into a fashion icon. No cosmetic or hair grooming commercial ever put more attention to detail or was photographed with more style and flair. We quickly discovered that little girls noticed and appreciated the difference. Special techniques were developed to make Barbie look glamorous under hot lights and through the eye of the camera. Filming a close-up of a beautiful woman has its own set of problems, but when the model's head is the size of a quail's egg, enormous difficulties arise. Not to speak of what happens to plastic material under hot lights. Eventually we learned through trial and error. We froze the dolls overnight so they wouldn't melt under the lights the next day. We learned to keep hair and fashion stylists on the sets to daub the hairdos with water and make sure the clothes fit smartly.

Barbie became an overnight success, and in 1958 when the doll was introduced television exposure was deliberately curtailed because Mattel quickly discovered the doll was going to be in short supply.

The following year the demand also exceeded the supply and the toy industry accused Mattel of holding back shipments as a selling tactic to keep the trade hungry and prolong the life of the doll. This, of course, was nonsense. The method of manufacture in Japan was laborious, and consumer demand for the product was totally unprecedented.

Of all the costumes Barbie has had over the years—and there have been hundreds—one of the best-selling was established early. It was Barbie's Wedding Gown which originally sold for $5.00, more than the price of the doll. Mattel soon realized that a bridal gown wasn't much good without a groom and perhaps Barbie needed a boyfriend, or at the very least, a fantasy escort. Perhaps little girls might even have as much fun dressing up a boy as they did Barbie.

The first models of Ken (named after the Handler's son) were not too much different from today's Ken. Mattel was careful to give him boyish, clean-cut looks and the overall, non-threatening, asexual appearance of a wimpy little jerk. His androgenous looks and his lack of sexual equipment immediately became a hot internal issue.

Perhaps Ken's anatomy would not have been such an important consideration had it not been for the fact that Barbie's breasts were so fundamental to her appeal. (If Barbie were blown up to human size, her measurements would be 39-21-33.) The breasts were necessary for realism and to allow Barbie's costumes to hang properly, but of course the breasts became more than that in little girls' fantasies of growing up.

The burning question at Mattel now became how real, how explicit should they make Ken. If his genitalia were included, some mothers would object. If his genitalia were omitted, would he look like some wounded Hemingway hero? Would mothers think we were putting our heads in the sand? Were we going to be accused of sexism, another issue brewing at that time?

The matter was so confusing they decided to consult a psychologist. The leading one in the world of marketing was Dr. Ernest Dichter. Dr. Dichter, who coined the phrase and the technique of motivational research, was a hot item on Madison Avenue in those years. He conducted his experiments at his laboratories at Croton-on-Hudson, and was hired by industry on day rates as a consultant on thorny and complex issues.

After observing a sample of little girls playing with Barbie dolls at his laboratories, Dr. Dichter came to California to consult with the Handlers, the toy marketing group, and the advertising agency. We spent a morning with Dr. Dichter discussing the problem. He pointed out that the primary play mode for the Barbie and Ken dolls was dressing and undressing them. He questioned whether children would understand that Ken was a boyfriend, or comprehend what a boyfriend really was. Would they see Ken as their fathers, brothers, or the boy next door? And if so, was it healthy to see him undressed? And when he was naked, why did he or didn't he look like Daddy or a brother?

The solution, like most solutions made by a committee, was a compromise. It was agreed that Ken would be molded in a permanent set of jockey shorts with a lump in the appropriate spot. No curious little girl would ever be able to remove his underwear.

That might have been a fine solution, except that somehow in the manufacturing process in Japan, one of the engineering supervisors determined that molding on the shorts was too difficult and that the lump added about a cent and a half worth of plastic to the product, so he arbitrarily eliminated both.

Ken was brought into the world as a neuter and it didn't matter one whit. Barbie's virginity was not threatened. Children did not think Ken had been in some horrible accident. Those issues had all been concerns of adults who had over-stressed the problem. Ken was, and still is, accepted as a necessary escort to many of Barbie's activities. There was a lesson in this for all of us: do not substitute your own tastes, thoughts, or imagination for a child's.

With the advent of Ken, a richer story in Barbie's life blossomed. It was easier to take Barbie on her 60-second (later 30-second) television adventures when an escort was involved. Her activities became virtually unlimited. Each commercial was treated as a mini-episode in Barbie's glamorous life. It became astonishing to us that little girls could learn so much about a celebrity in such short informational doses. Of course, only hints were necessary. The girls supplied the rest through their young, active imaginations.

In the earliest versions of Barbie and her costumes, Mattel included a tiny folded pamphlet showing some of the highlights of Barbie's wardrobe. The pamphlet also included an address where girls could write to Barbie. A newsletter response was promised from time to time. The reaction to this write-in was enormous and after a few issues of an inexpensive all-type newsletter, we converted to a two-color magazine. The agency prepared the magazine once every two months and packed it solid with fashion tips for girls, ideas for things they could make at home, simple and fun recipes, puzzles, and probably best of all, fictional tales about Barbie.

Creating the magazine was a new and interesting experience for some of the women art directors and writers working at Carson/Roberts. As they prepared each article and fashion illustration, it appeared that they relived their childhood doll-playing years. These were the same cynical professionals who were creating high fashion advertising for Max Factor cosmetics, Vassarette bras, and Rose Marie Reid swimsuits. Of course, what tickled them even more was that Random House bought their material separately for a series of Barbie books.

The Barbie Magazine became an instant hit and it paved the way to an even bigger idea—the Barbie Fan Club. The fan club began with writing Barbie for her newsletter or magazine, but its biggest push came through television.

We prepared a television commercial in a style that might be called cinema verite today. We had noticed that the young actresses we used for Barbie commercials had a tendency to mug before the camera which lent a subtle but noticeable note of artificiality. We wanted a more realistic commercial using a few of these eight-year-old thespians but were concerned they would all try to upstage one another. On a fairly conventional, secretly miked movie set we included the standard 35 mm. camera and a cameraman. Unknown to the actresses, the main camera was empty. Several cinematographers walked around the set with hand-held cameras and filmed the events as they happened. We merely asked the girls to have a Barbie party and they created scenes we could never have staged. They found ways for Barbie and Ken to dance together, to duplicate shots from the magazine, and to play with the dolls as their imaginations dictated. The results were entirely natural. And when this commercial appeared on television, the results were astounding.

The direct response to an invitation to join the Barbie Fan Club was unprecedented. This commercial received more response than any previous commercial in the first 25 years of television.

The fan club was eventually set up everywhere in the world with a fulfillment company in Amsterdam that answered Barbie's mail in 16 different languages. The Barbie Fan Club became the second largest girl's organization in the world after the Girl Scouts.

In those early years when Mattel encouraged write-ins, Barbie received more fan mail than any other celebrity. She averaged over 10,000 letters a week. Only Shirley Temple had more. Her record of 65,000 letters a month during the mid-'30s still stands.

Naturally, copies of the Barbie doll appeared. The toy industry is notorious for producing copies of successful products. In the parlance of the toy trade, these are called knockoffs. There were cheap Hong Kong manufactured knockoffs, quality knockoffs, there were knockoffs of younger versions of Barbie without breasts, and knockoffs of older versions with even more noticeable bosoms. None were really successful. One of the tactics we used to counter knockoffs was a tag placed on Barbie's wrist

60 SECONDS

1. (SFX: GIRLS LAUGHING/ PLAYING)

2. ANNCR: This is an Official Barbie Fan Club Chapter Meeting.

3. (MUSIC UNDER) Barbie invites you to join and it's free.

4. When you belong, you can form a chapter with your friends

5. for all the fun of meeting together.

6. During your meetings, you might share a story about Barbie, Ken and Midge

7. from the Barbie Magazine.

8. Mattel's Official Barbie Fan Club is free.

9. To join, pick up an application blank at your toy store

10. or write Barbie, Post Office Box 44, Los Angeles 51, California.

11. Barbie will send you a letter about the fan club; news about the Barbie Magazine,

12. your official Club Membership Card

13. and your own Barbie Fan Club Badge.

14. Write Barbie, Post Office Box 44,

15. Los Angeles 51, California.

The Barbie Fan Club commercial was created in cinema verite style. This commercial drew more response from children than any commercial in the first 25 years of television. (Courtesy, Mattel, Inc.)

indicating she was the one and only original Barbie. We brought children's attention to the tag on television so they would be sure to know which was which.

In fighting the competitive knockoffs, we learned several important things. When you have an original product, stress its originality with such things as a tag on the wrist, a newsletter or magazine, or a fan club. These activities protect the originality of your product.

We learned that children have more product loyalty than adults. Children and their mothers, when shopping for a Barbie doll, would visit more than one store if the product were out of stock. In fact, they continued to shop until they found what they wanted.

There have been numerous efforts by other major toy companies to compete with Barbie in the fashion doll category, to take a portion of this market which Barbie has dominated for almost 30 years. Some of these efforts have been substantially funded, and in at least one instance, Dawn, made by Topper, the expenditures on television advertising exceeded those of Mattel for Barbie. Other major competitors have been the Chrissy doll with long, flowing hair; Dusty, an athletic version of Barbie; and the celebrity dolls such as Farrah Fawcett, Cher, Charlie's Angels, and Brooke Shields.

At this writing, Hasbro, the current leader of the U.S. toy industry, has introduced Jem, a new fashion doll with punk rock purple hair and outfits like Madonna's. Jem also has her very own rock band, called the Holograms. She also has her own half-hour animated television series that has been successfully launched in syndication. No one, including Hasbro, believes that Jem will push Barbie off the market, but at the moment Barbie is facing the most formidable competition of her career.

One of the reasons Barbie has survived on top for so many years is that Mattel has had the foresight to update Barbie to keep with the competition and the times. On the heels of Jem, Mattel is now combing the nation for a young woman who can play the role of Barbie in a band called Barbie and the Rockers. They are also creating a new Barbie magazine-type television show.

In a recent interview with Bob Howard of the *Los Angeles Business Journal*, Ruth Handler, who left Mattel with her husband in 1974, said that she believes turning Barbie into a reality is a bad thing to do. "I considered having a real Barbie years ago but rejected the idea very strongly because I do not feel it is good to give Barbie a specific personality." The problem with a real life Barbie, Ruth Handler says, is that she might limit the imaginations of girls who play with the dolls. "Barbie has lasted 27 years because she has had no specific personality. Each little girl has her own dreams about who Barbie is, whether she's a career woman or a housewife or whatever. If you give her a specific personality, it could mean that little girls will lose their ability to project whatever personalities they want onto Barbie."

The original idea for keeping Barbie updated was probably first discovered in 1963 when Barbie sales began to plateau. Market research at that time indicated that Barbie had virtually saturated the market. In affluent communities the ownership of one or more Barbie dolls was virtually 95 percent. In upper middle-class markets ownership among girls four to eight years of age was 80 percent.

Research also showed that girls in the target market, four to eight, usually played with their Barbies for 18 months before they tired of her. In addition, research indicated that girls bought about two and a half costumes for every doll owned and that costumes were most likely bought immediately after purchase or ownership of a new doll. Mattel then realized that the number of new girls coming into the market each year (less than two million) could not sustain the spectacular growth of new doll ownership, and without new dolls, costume sales slowed down to a walk. Mattel found itself in a razor and razor blade business in which new dolls had to be introduced every year or so to sell costumes.

It was at that time that two ideas were formed to stage what turned out to be one of toy history's most successful promotions. In the '60s, Barbie's overall appearance began to look dated. Her face makeup and hairdos began to look like Joan Crawford in the 1940s. She had a hard bitchy look that was a far cry from the healthy sun-tanned look of the glamorous new teenagers. Her zebra-striped swimsuit was also hopelessly outdated by newer, sexier fashions.

Mattel brought out a brand-new, suntanned, natural looking Barbie with a waist mechanism that allowed her body to "twist 'n turn" to strike more natural poses. Her basic costume became a new orange swimsuit with see-through mesh at the waist, accentuating her new feature.

The only problem with bringing out a new Barbie doll was the extensive ownership of the old model. Would girls want the new doll if they already had an old one? This question gave rise to a promotion known as the Barbie Trade-in. Here's the way it worked: Mattel sold 1,250,000 new Twist 'n Turn dolls to the trade. These dolls were specially packaged and marked for sale at $1.50, less than half the regular price. Mattel made no profit on these introductory dolls and the retailer realized $.25 on each unit.

The television commercial opens by showing the all-new Barbie, emphasizing her new sun-tanned look and her Twist 'n Turn waist.

1. (MUSIC UNDER) MAN: Have you heard what's happened? Barbie's changed.

2. Barbie's new and different. She's the very same size, but now she comes with a groovy outdoor look.

3. And Barbie's lashes are really for real and even her face has changed.

4. (MUSIC)

5. Best of all the biggest news of all is the way Barbie moves. The new Barbie twists, the new Barbie turns.

6. Wouldn't you like the new Barbie.

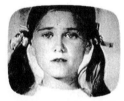

7. GIRL: But what do I do with my old Barbie?

8. MAN: What do you do? Here's what you do,

9. just take your old Barbie before it's too late and run, run, run to the toy store.

10. Then trade it to the man with the $1.50. Less than half what you'd normally pay

11. and look what you get. New Barbie for less than half price.

12. Better hurry up, first come, first serve. There's a limited supply at this special low price,

13. so take your old Barbie and a dollar and a half

14. and trade 'em for the Barbie who's new.

15. GIRL: Trade in your old Barbie today while you can still get the new Barbie less than half price.

The Barbie Trade-In was one of the most successful promotions in toy history. Mattel sold 1,250,000 new dolls within a couple of months. The promotion introduced a new Twist n' Turn Barbie. (Courtesy, Mattel Inc.)

35

Suddenly a forelorn looking girl appears holding her old Barbie doll and asks "But what do I do with my old Barbie?" The commercial then jumps into high gear with explicit instructions to girls telling them, "Here's what you do. You take your old Barbie plus $1.50 to the toy store and trade it in for the Barbie who's new." Urgency is added by showing a line of girls skipping hurriedly to the toy store to get the new Barbie "while supplies last at the introductory low price."

With such a short selling season, not much time existed to test this radical idea on television. We were forced to test the commercial on the air in February, a month in which very few toys are sold. We tested in two markets in the Middle West. On the first Saturday the commercial was introduced, there was heavy snow in both markets. In one city the blizzard was so bad it blocked television reception; yet, within two weeks, we knew the idea was a success. Girls and their mothers went out in the snow to purchase the new dolls. Both test markets were sold out in three weeks. Well before the last quarter of that year, all 1,250,000 introductory dolls were sold and by Christmas the new Barbie doll returned to its regular price to achieve record sales in units sold in one year. The erosion of Barbie sales which had started to occur had been reversed and the product was now selling again in introductory proportions. Sales have never flagged again to this very day. Costume sales continue to make Mattel the largest manufacturer of women's wear in the world.

Since that time, Barbie has seen many different looks. She had bendable legs. There was and still is a deeply sun-tanned Barbie called Malibu Barbie. There was a very glamorous Super Star Barbie. And today there is a busy Career Girl Barbie, reflecting the new work force of young women in the United States.

Mattel not only continually tests the wind for new currents of fashion and social change, but continually tries new looks for Barbie in concept form. The testing procedure is simple, but reliable. Concept boards are prepared showing Barbie in a main illustration. Smaller illustrations around her enhance the point being made by other aspects of the life-style shown in the primary or major illustrations. The boards are then shown to children who are asked, "Which of these do you prefer?" Results are usually quite clear.

The trends that exist in the United States do not always exist elsewhere at the same time. Sometimes it takes several years for other countries to catch up, if they catch up at all. Consequently, Mattel's international Barbie line does not exactly parallel the products in the United States. Nevertheless, Barbie is a big seller overseas.

Barbie was first introduced in Europe in 1962. The Germans thought it was Lili and rejected the product out of hand. The French thought the product was too American. Mattel's distributor in Sweden wouldn't even handle the line. And the British preferred a copy of Barbie without breasts.

Only with years of perseverance did Mattel finally overcome the objections of a conservative and stubborn European toy industry. In almost every case, once the trade stocked the doll and displayed it on shelves, children did the rest. The early negative reactions to Barbie from conservative adults were absolutely astonishing, especially in light of highly favorable children's reactions.

Today, little girls all over the world (except in Japan where girls prefer a Eurasian doll) have responded enthusiastically to Barbie and in a way no other children's product has yet matched.

The lesson we learned here, of course, was that parental or adult negatives can be overcome if the child wants the product badly enough (and if the product is safe).

The Shtick Dolls

Barbie paved the way for Mattel in the doll business, one of the toy industry's major categories. This part of the toy industry had been dominated year in and year out by Madame Alexander on the high quality end of the spectrum and Ideal in the more popularly priced area. Ideal had the Shirley Temple dolls during the '30s and made dolls a primary source of their business. There were at least a dozen companies in the field, all making some form of baby doll.

Differentiation, except for sleeping or wetting, was not great. The basic appeal of the child playing mother to a doll was all pretty much the same. Differences were established in looks, clothing, price, and quality of manufacture.

Two types of technology changed the doll business forever: television, with its ability to demonstrate, and a clear, precise talking mechanism that Mattel inserted into their first big doll. The first talking doll, Chatty Cathy, said 11 different things, at random. She said them audibly and clearly whenever you pulled her Chatty Ring. And boy, did she talk on television. She talked business, too. She sold herself on television to more than 1,000,000 little girls the first year she appeared on the scene. No one had ever before sold a million units of any toy priced over $10.

In testing and ongoing observations of children with Chatty Cathy, it became apparent that the talking mechanism was relatively unimportant *after* the doll was purchased. Girls quickly tired of the talking novelty and went back to playing with Chatty as if she were any other baby doll. Ultimately the talking feature was only important to make her more attractive on television.

Mattel assumed that if a little talking was important to the doll's appeal, then a lot of talking might be even better. The next version of the doll became a smart alec little pixie named Charmin' Chatty. She could say *hundreds* of different things and say many of them in Spanish and in French. While the talking mechanism was obviously new and improved, the new smartie look that went with such an intelligent little creature left the kids absolutely cold. They hated her glasses and her snobbish attitude. They didn't want a doll for a friend, even a smart friend. They wanted a doll who was still a baby and only learning to talk. No amount of television advertising could move Charmin' Chatty off the shelves. Mattel experienced its first expensive flop. Television demonstration and heavy advertising simply could not move a product with a poor concept.

Mattel quickly returned to baby dolls and Chatty Cathy was followed by Chatty Baby, a doll that could gurgle, coo, and cry. Her sales exceeded the original Chatty Cathy. Sound was not the only innovation added to a subsequently long parade of baby dolls with a special new feature, or as they say in show business, a new shtick or piece of business. Mattel and others ushered forth dolls that wet, cried real tears, laughed, walked, crawled, burped, walked on their tip toes, rode tricycles, roller-skated, and defecated into changeable diapers.

There was even a ballerina baby doll that could spin and pirouette. And finally, a return to a doll that did nothing except let you feel her lifelike skin. Television made it all possible to demonstrate, adding a new play dimension to a product category that had been around for ages.

THE SUPERSPIES

As television programming goes, so goes the toy industry. What is hot on television shows up almost immediately as a toy. Mattel had already discovered this with Mickey Mouse products and Western toys. After the Westerns came the cops and robbers shows, and Mattel had a brief fling with some Dick Tracy products when Dick Tracy returned to television in animation. Cops and robbers had never been a particularly appealing genre for children. By the early '60s, however, the cops and robbers genre had taken a new twist. Inspired by the first James Bond movies, television brought forth "The Man From U.N.C.L.E." and "I Spy." The research we did indicated that James Bond was, by far, the most popular agent with kids and adults. Research told us that boys loved Bond, but not because of his suave manner, expertise with women, or even his exploits. What they loved was his spy gear. Bond's Aston-Martin, with all its various hidden tricks, was a big thrill for boys, as were all the other seemingly ordinary items (like briefcases or watches) that turned into weapons.

Mattel's first interest was to obtain a license to make an action line of James Bond merchandise. At the time, Ian Fleming, author of the original James Bond books, was still alive and he refused the Bond license to anyone. He did not want to commercialize what he considered serious literature.

Mattel had already developed merchandise for a line of spy toys: a camera that turned into a cap pistol, a pen that could squirt water and write text visible only to those with special glasses, and a portable radio that turned into a cap-firing automatic rifle. Without the James Bond name on the product, they needed another merchandising hook.

The problem was turned over to the advertising agency. We invented a secret agent of our own—one who existed only in a boy's fantasy. He was called Agent Zero M. The name was an obvious derivative of Bond's "007" and his superior, "M." But, when written, the "Zero M" contained a circle enclosing the M that resembled the Mattel logotype.

Agent Zero M, as you saw him on television, was a boy secret agent. In the commercials, an ordinary boy daydreams while doing homework or mowing the lawn, and suddenly imagines himself as a secret agent using Mattel's "Snap-Shot" pistol or "Radio Rifle."

When these commercials were placed on television, Mattel was suddenly faced with heavy competition in the category. Ideal Toys had "Man From U.N.C.L.E." products. Topper, always following Mattel, brought out their own agent, Secret Sam. And as fate would have it, Fleming died and his estate licensed the James Bond name to Multiple Toys.

Over the next two seasons however, the competition hardly mattered. Agent Zero M was far and away the most popular and best-selling of the bunch. These toys became among Mattel's biggest hits. The superspy fad was a short lived one, but Mattel was right on top of it.

More than any other factor, the success of these products depended on their television presentation. Other companies had similar merchandise, but none of them were so able to capture the essence of the superspy adventures in their television advertising.

The boy we cast as Agent Zero M had already been signed by Disney for the movies, but had not yet appeared in anything popular. His name

60 SECONDS

1. MOM: (VO) Finished your homework yet? BOY: Yes, Mom.

2. (MUSIC) If she only knew the secret briefing session waiting for me. Agent Zero M.

3. I'm ready, sir.

4. MAN: Splendid. You will need certain special equipment.

5. MAN: First this portable radio, or so it seems.

6. BOY: Yes? MAN: Show him the Zero M Radio Rifle. (SFX)

7. Created especially for counter espionage by Mattel.

8. MAN: The Zero M Jet Coder.

9. Write the secret message you can see only with these glasses. And if you get in a jam...

10. This is the Zero M Snapshot.

11. MAN: Well named.

12. MAN: Press here and the snapshot.

13. MAN: You see, it's not the camera. All three come in this special Zero M Weapon Set by Mattel.

14. MAN: Or separately, of course.

15. MAN: We cleverly place them wherever toys are sold for agents who might need extras.

16. MAN: You know the password.

17. BOY: Zero M.

18. MAN: Correct. You leave immediately?

19. BOY: Right after school.

20. (CHATTER/MUSIC OUT)

Mattel's Zero M was a boy secret agent made popular by television commercials. Each commercial was a boy's fantasy. Here he is in a briefing session with some sinister looking types. (Courtesy, Mattel Inc.)

was Kurt Russell and at the time he was nine years old. He has since become a famous Hollywood star. To make Agent Zero M fantasies take on the look of a Bond movie, we took Kurt to Cary Grant's tailor and fitted him for a tuxedo and a trench coat. We placed him in settings that looked like Monte Carlo or in briefing sessions with sinister looking adults. Even as a child, Kurt could act. His facial expressions, voice, and mannerisms epitomized the James Bond cool.

When Kurt had the time, he appeared at department stores in his familiar trenchcoat to sign autographs for kids and to give out secret Zero M tattoos. For a brief few months his television commercials made him more famous with kids than Bond himself.

In many ways these early Zero M commercials and the secret agent as hero concept opened the way for a series of male action products to come. Mattel followed the superspy fad with space. The hero was a small male action figure called Major Matt Mason. He was an astronaut in space using various space vehicles for space explorations. Despite his attributes, he was a flop.

We quickly discovered it was easy for boys to play cowboys and Indians, cops and robbers, superspies against bad guys, but there were no adversaries beyond the elements in the modern concept of space. The bad guys or evil aliens had to be created. The creators of Flash Gordon and Buck Rogers, who had explored space adventures earlier, knew what they were doing. In any male action toy category the fantasy story projected must be the conflict of good versus evil.

That fantasy is so deeply ingrained in our culture that no other story line works. From generation to generation, children never tire of it.

THE FASTEST CARS IN THE WORLD

Mattel was relentless in its pursuit of new toy categories to enter. They discovered that the way to enter a category was to find a technical innovation that improved existing products and advertise it heavily on television, quickly making the other products on the market obsolete. The modus operandi was to jump in quickly, lead, then dominate.

Hot Wheels was such a case. Miniature die-cast metal cars had been around for years. The industry knew them as Matchbox cars, although only one company, Lesney, owns the "Matchbox" name. Lesney is a conservative British company who enjoyed a comfortable world-wide business making and selling their little replicas of classic automobiles. In

1. (WIND BLOWING) ANNCR: (VO) Setting up

2. on location

3. to show you how far,

4. how fast Sizzlers move

5. even in brutal 115 degree desert heat. Hot Wheels Sizzlers.

6. Charged with the juice machine;

7. ready to roll on three football fields

8. of track,

9. flat out.

10. (MUSIC)

11. (MUSIC)

12. (MUSIC)

13. (MUSIC)

14. (MUSIC)

15. Sizzlers from Mattel. The fastest Hot Wheels yet.

Mattel's Hot Wheels cars revolutionized the die-cast metal car category in the toy industry. Television commercials allowed children to see just how far and how fast Hot Wheels cars could go. (Courtesy, Mattel Inc.)

fact, they were an institution of sorts, and from the looks of their distribution in tobacconists, newsstands, and gift shops as well as toy stores, it appeared their cars were collected by as many grown men as little boys.

The young California engineers in Mattel's research and development department produced two innovations simultaneously.

Instead of Lesney's traditional classic cars, Mattel brought out racy new cars with California custom styling. In addition, the cars not only looked fast, they were fast. These new little cars were made with friction-free wheels that could run on plastic track. Gravity was the only energy force they needed, and when gravity was helped by a push or later, various propelling devices, the cars moved on the track with blinding speed. They were appropriately named "Hot Wheels."

The entire die-cast metal car market in the United States in 1967 was $23 million and Lesney had most of it. In 1968, Mattel's first year of Hot Wheels, they did $25 million in sales on this line. They almost put Lesney out of business in the United States, and later when they introduced Hot Wheels in Britain, had it not been for an outraged British press that believed a Yankee intruder had assaulted one of their hallowed institutions, Mattel would have chased Lesney out of the business it had founded.

Incidentally, it was never Mattel management's intention to hurt any of the older, more staid businesses in the toy industry. The Handlers looked upon many of these companies with a certain reverence. Their attitude was always one of expanding an existing market by product innovation and television advertising; however, they had such a headstart in their knowledge of marketing through television that it took many years for the industry to catch up. Until then, Mattel was an invincible competitor.

The Hot Wheels category started with a few cars and some simple track layouts. As the category grew, hundreds of cars and dozens of track sets on which the cars could race and go through mazes, curves, and loops with spectacular speed were developed. The cars were no longer just attractive little collectibles, the category became racing and speed, with power the all-important appeal.

Mattel did not have the racing category to itself for long. An upstart company in the East, named Topper, introduced a line of similar products called Johnny Lightning.

A European immigrant, Henry Orenstein, started Topper. He was tough, smart, and bold. He looked at Mattel's methods for success and copied the formula. He copied Barbie with Dawn; he copied Hot Wheels with Johnny Lightning; he matched Mattel dollar for dollar on television. In some cases he even outspent Mattel.

The competition on television, particularly between Hot Wheels and

Johnny Lightning, became fierce. Each company claimed more speed than the other; the cars in the television commercials looked impossibly fast. Both companies were doctoring their commercials, but few people realized that the cars were not sped up in the commercials. *They were slowed down.* The camera simply could not record them at their natural speed. What's more, the camera's eye was often placed where a human's eye might be, at the edge of the track. This made the cars coming around curves or jumping the track look very dramatic. As a result, some television viewers didn't believe either company's commercials and complaints filtered down to the Federal Trade Commission (FTC).

At the time a movement was growing inside the FTC itself. Several zealous new attorneys who had joined the commission believed the FTC had been too relaxed on children's television advertising. They were determined to show children's advertisers that the FTC had some teeth and they jumped into the Mattel-Topper issue with unprecedented zeal.

Both companies were cited. Both companies were tried in the press. The FTC refused to produce any of the so-called complaints and privately admitted they had not even seen the commercials before the citations were issued. They felt the toy industry was filled with dishonest advertising so they adopted a new strategy. Their technique was to bring the leader to its knees, hoping the other companies would learn by example.

Both Mattel and Topper were asked to sign consent orders. These were tantamount to promising not to beat your wife. While there was no concrete evidence of wife beating in the past, it was virtually a promise not to do it in the future. The promise included pledges not to speed up the cars on film, use odd lenses, or overly dramatic camera angles.

Mattel's attorneys and Carson/Roberts' attorneys advised us to sign the consent. They felt it was harmless and would not hurt business. What's more, to decline would mean expensive and drawn out litigation in the courts. I signed it reluctantly.

Had I the opportunity to relive the experience I wouldn't have signed it at gunpoint. I would have fought it through the courts to the end. On principle, I believe it was unfair strong-arming. Mattel has since regretted their own compliance. Years ago they discovered that every other company that put toy cars or racing on television could use camera techniques not permitted to them. How unfair can it get? They have since complained to the FTC and are trying to have the consent rescinded. Topper eventually went bankrupt trying to outspend Mattel and the issue is obviously no longer important to them.

During the hey day of Hot Wheels, Mattel ran afoul of the government—this time the Federal Communications Commission.

Since Hot Wheels was a hot topic for boys in those days, and custom cars, souped up engines, racing, and all the other lore surrounding hot rodding was at its height of popularity, it was only natural a children's show be developed around the subject. My colleague at the agency, Eddie Smardan, was an experienced producer of children's programs and he joined forces with Ken Snyder, another producer, to create "The Hot Wheels" show for kids. Obviously, Mattel had a financial interest in the program. ABC bought the show on its own merits and programmed it for Saturday morning. Mattel was permitted a sponsorship, but was not allowed to run Hot Wheels commercials within the show. This was one of the earliest examples of the "half-hour commercial" about which more is discussed in a later chapter.

A show developed around a line of preexisting children's products appeared to many as overcommercialization and was brought to the FCC's attention. After a suitable investigation and explanation from ABC, the FCC dropped the matter with a vague warning about future ventures of this sort. In due time, "Hot Wheels" was dropped from ABC's Saturday morning schedule to create time for the fad of another season.

Perhaps the incident is only interesting because it has again arisen in full force. Many shows of this kind are currently on the air and the FCC has been asked to reconsider the question.

THE TOY INDUSTRY MATURES

During the years between 1955 and 1970, the toy industry grew remarkably. Mattel had pioneered the way to an entirely new kind of industry in which television advertising became as important as new products. The structure of the industry changed as well. Once dominated by wholesalers who were essentially the largest customers for a manufacturer, the big retail discount chains entered the business in force and started to buy and warehouse product at the same price as the wholesalers. By 1970, the large toy wholesalers, or jobbers, as they were called, became dinosaurs. The largest and best known ones went out of business entirely. Television's ability to demonstrate toys had enabled the toy manufacturers to turn directly to the consumer for judgment, rather than have a product judged by a wholesale toy buyer for its selling appeal.

If television could sell it off the shelves in the mass discount stores, the trade stocked it heavily and the product was a hit.

This industry could now legitimately hold itself against the more sophisticated industries in packaged goods such as cereals, candy, chewing gum, and soft drinks that were brand oriented and had learned long before how to make their products popular with children. Toy advertising budgets became very substantial in comparison. In a 15-year period, Mattel's budget went from $150,000 to $15 million. In fact, it was the size of that budget that helped Carson/Roberts grow and become one of the largest independent advertising agencies west of the Mississippi.

CARSON/ROBERTS BECOMES OGILVY & MATHER AND OUR CHILDREN'S WORLD EXPANDS

By 1970 Carson/Roberts had been through 15 heady years with Mattel. Those years enveloped the most exciting and historically important growth story in children's advertising. The agency acquired a reputation as one of the experts in the field of children's advertising. Back east, Dancer Fitzgerald Sample had great success with General Mills cereals, Grey had successfully advertised Kool-Aid and Ideal Toys, and the Leo Burnett agency in Chicago had done an outstanding job for Kellogg's. Being thought of in that company, for a small West Coast agency, was considered unusual and unprecedented. Our creative reputation turned us into a rare jewel many larger agencies now wanted to acquire. And many came courting.

At the same time Mattel's business overseas had begun to grow. They entered into Europe and the rest of the world in 1962 and were rapidly expanding. We set up a network of affiliate agencies in Europe, Canada, and Australia and put several people overseas to coordinate international affairs. In addition, Mattel established a game company in New Jersey that required special attention. It became increasingly apparent that Mattel's growing needs required the strength and breadth of a large international agency that could service them anywhere. We were faced with two choices—let some of that business go its own way and try to keep what we had in Los Angeles, or sell out to a big agency and try to control it all. We chose the latter, and in December 1970 we announced that Carson/Roberts had been sold to Ogilvy & Mather, one of the top 10 agencies in the world.

The founding partners, Ralph Carson and Jack Roberts, who had not been very active for several years prior to the merger, retired entirely from agency life. I stayed on to continue managing the agency and Mattel's affairs. However, I now had some new bosses, some new mentors, and some new associates—all anxious to use our experience in children's advertising to acquire more business in that field.

I quickly learned that the enormous success attained by Ogilvy & Mather as a leading worldwide agency was not solely due to David Ogilvy's ability as a creative adman. His real genius was as an advertising philosopher, a charming showman, and a great teacher and editor. David Ogilvy's experience as a researcher and a creative man gave way to some principles and points of view that affected Ogilvy & Mather profoundly and have endured to this day.

In his desire to make Ogilvy & Mather "the agency who knows the most about advertising," Ogilvy developed internal systems for gathering information on a subject, codifying it, putting it in interesting presentation form, and then disseminating it throughout the organization. The agency then used this special information or presentation to approach prospects and impress them with the agency's knowledge of their businesses. These special presentations, mostly on slides and video tape, are referred to as lanterns, a name derived from David Ogilvy's original presentation on "How to Create Successful Advertising" because Ogilvy called it his "Magic Lantern Show." The agency has dozens of these presentations and they have become the corpus of knowledge upon which the agency was built.

After becoming part of Ogilvy & Mather, I was asked to develop a magic lantern on children's advertising, incorporating all I had learned in the 15 years of working on Mattel. That was the infant and the inspiration for this book.

The presentation I subsequently developed on "How to Advertise to Children," became an important tool for acquiring new business from existing Ogilvy accounts and new clients. Over the next few years the presentation helped win some additional assignments from Hershey's, some promotional assignments on Kool-Aid and other soft drinks and candy projects from General Foods, the introduction of Cookie Crisp cereals from Ralston, the Burger Chef fast food restaurants from General Foods, a fruit candy from Del Monte, and ultimately four different children's cereal brands from General Foods, a category that Ogilvy had been coveting for years. The presentation was also used to acquire the children's advertising for Aim Toothpaste from Lever Bros., more Mattel business in many different countries, an ice cream account in Italy, the introduction of soft bubble gum in France and Brazil, the Kool-Aid brand in a half-dozen countries; and Estrella, the leading toy company in Brazil.

Most importantly for me, Ogilvy & Mather's vast network of contacts with major advertisers gave me and a handful of associates in Los Angeles a much larger stage and we were able to build on our earlier experiences by working on many different brands in all the children's categories. Most of Ogilvy's new children's advertising assignments subsequently flowed into the Los Angeles office, where a cadre of experienced and talented creative people learned their children's advertising lessons working on Mattel.

THE PRODUCT AS PERSONALITY IN CANDY FORM

One of our first, and most delicious assignments, came from Hershey's. The campaign was to introduce Rolos, a mound-shaped chocolate covered caramel which came in a cardboard tube. While the packaging was somewhat innovative, there was nothing especially interesting about the candy itself. Hershey's chocolate products are high quality and rank well with chocolate lovers everywhere, but there were many chocolate products on the market and we had to find a way to differentiate this one for children.

Instead of using a conventional taste strategy emphasizing the delicious taste of the chocolate, the chewiness of the caramels, even how fresh the candy stayed in the new handy tube, we decided to make the candy look like a lot more fun than it appeared to be on first blush.

Russ Alben, one of our creative directors and a Mattel veteran who had worked on toy and cereal accounts in the East, developed a very funny approach. He made the chocolate-covered caramels into The Dancing Rolos.

In the commercial, five dancers in mound-shaped, chocolate-covered suits, came dancing out of tubes and put on a vaudeville dance act. Except the suits were clumsy, they couldn't dance, and they fell all over themselves trying to look good. The effect was pure slapstick comedy and children thought the product would be fun to eat—paramount when introducing a new product. From our point of view, it was another example of positioning the product as a personality, a strategy that seemed highly successful with children. The leap from humanizing an 11½ inch fashion doll to humanizing some chocolate drops was not as great as one might think.

Burger Chef and Jeff, the Dynamic Duo of the Hamburger World

In the early '70s, General Foods had purchased a chain of fast food hamburger restaurants operated primarily in the Midwest and South. The chain was very much like McDonalds or Burger King, without the savvy, service, or promotional drive.

Headquartered in Indianapolis and managed by General Foods packaged goods executives who were isolated from the GF mainstream in White Plains, New York, the business was bleeding red ink. Morale was poor, and the smell of doom enveloped the entire enterprise. GF decided they needed a new advertising agency that could breathe some life into the company. They asked Ogilvy & Mather to take it on. No agency likes to associate itself with terminal cases, but GF was a highly treasured client for Ogilvy and we reckoned that the Burger Chef business had only one way to go, and that was up. A failure at this late stage would not shame us. With luck, we could be heroes.

We decided to handle it as a team comprised of New York office account management and Los Angeles creative and promotion. Los Angeles was chosen once again for its expertise in the children's field and because we also understood the fast food business. We plunged in with a task force to turn the business around as quickly as possible. Our immediate recommendations were fundamental: close the unprofitable stores and concentrate the promotional dollars in markets where stores were doing better. About 40 percent of the stores were discontinued, taking the number to about 550, all in the Midwest. The remaining recommendations were also simple: wash the windows, sweep the floors, and get the hamburgers hot. Let us do the rest.

We immediately determined that management and the previous agency had not read the research correctly. They believed that only adults made the decision to eat in a Burger Chef, a McDonalds, or a Burger King. That was only half right. Parents made the decision to go out to eat. Once out, the kids then militated for their favorite place to go. If the place were clean and the food palatable, the parents would give in to the kids' desires. We believed we could convince kids more quickly than adults that Burger Chef was a fun place to go.

Strangely enough, for a restaurant called Burger Chef, there was no pictorial image of a chef. So we invented one. He was a cartoon version of a jolly, friendly, portly chef whom kids would like. We gave him a teenage sidekick named Jeff for his eager assistant. Jeff added the important facet of youth to the new corporate personality (shades of the Lone Ranger and

1. (MUSIC UP)

2. (MUSIC UNDER) JEFF: Baffling bats, Burger Chef, what's that?

3. COUNT FANGBURGER: Count Fangburger

4. with my whole "fang-mily." (BAT LAUGHS)

5. MOTHER FANGBURGER: The little ones are unhappy, so we took them out for a bite. (BAT LAUGHS)

6. COUNT FANGBURGER: I could have a nibble myself.

7. JEFF: What do we do, Burger Chef? BURGER CHEF: Oh, never fear, Jeff. My Funburger is here.

8. BOY FANGBURGER: Oh, goody goody, this is fun.

9. (BAT LAUGHS)

10. GIRL FANGBURGER: Yeepee! Fun, fun, fun.

11. COUNT FANGBURGER: Burger Chef, what is the secret of your Funburger?

12. BURGER CHEF: Oh well, that's easy. (LAUGHS)

13. You see my Funburger is a delicious all beef burger with a smile on the wrapper.

14. And inside the funny Funburger box... (LAUGHS) is a surprise of a prize.

15. BOY FANGBURGER: Yeepee! Look what I got. GIRL FANGBURGER: Yeepee! Look what I got.

16. MOTHER FANGBURGER: Say "fang" you to the nice man.

17. BOY AND GIRL FANG-BURGER: Thanks a lot, Burger Chef.

18. (MUSIC AND SFX)

19. JEFF: Your Funburger is great,

20. and Burger Chef, you're incrediburgable! (BURGER CHEF LAUGHS)

Dracula is a monster that all kids understand and relate to. In this Burger Chef commercial he is changed into Count Fangburger who brings his whole "fang-mily" in for a bite. Burger Chef and Jeff serve them up a Funburger. (By permission of Burger Chef Systems, Inc./Hardee's Food Systems, Inc.)

Tonto, Dick Tracy and Junior, and Batman and Robin). This dynamic duo of the hamburger world became the hero spokesmen for the company. They appeared in animated commercials as hamburger heroes rescuing starving customers with quickly dished up delicious burgers, fries, and malts. A parade of unusual customers added an element of fun to the entirely new atmosphere of Burger Chef. One of those customers was a mock vampire named Count Fang Burger. He was in the habit of bringing in the whole Fangmily, including his wife and all the kiddie Draculas, just for "a bite." Other popular monsters, like Frankenstein and King Kong, became Burger Chef regulars.

In addition, we started merchandising hamburgers in a whole new way. Hamburgers were wrapped in a tissue with a smiling face. The burgers were delivered to the customer in a box imprinted with cartoons, puzzles, and games—things to do while eating or after. An ordinary hamburger was suddenly transformed into a "Fun Burger." Hamburgers, fries, and a drink came in cut out cardboard trays with similar entertainments. That became a "Fun Meal."

The new campaign took hold immediately and business increased dramatically. In markets where Burger Chef advertised, the "Funburger" stood alongside "The Big Mac" and "The Whopper" in popularity. Burger Chef and Jeff proved to be likeable spokesmen, immediately recognized as fun characters who gave the Burger Chef restaurants a singular identity.

The solution of creating a Burger Chef and Jeff was really not much different from creating a personality for a toy product kids would identify with and consequently like.

Incidentally, GF ultimately sold its Burger Chef interests and these stores have now become part of the Hardee's chain.

A MOVING PITCHER BECOMES A PRODUCT PERSONALITY

The management at General Foods realized they had an important creative resource in Los Angeles that could help them considerably with children's products. They started looking to us for more and more assistance on all manner of projects.

One of those projects was a series of development ideas for a carbonated Kool-Aid product. While none of the ideas we explored for carbonated Kool-Aid ever saw fruition, it did put us in an interesting position to

1. (MUSIC AND SFX: PLANES)

2. (MUSIC UNDER) BURGERRILLA: Burger Chef and Jeff. JEFF: It's Burgerrilla, the terribly unhappy ape.

3. BURGERRILLA: Nobody likes me.

4. WOMAN: Because you're no fun. BURGERRILLA: Oh, I'm not having any fun.

5. JEFF: Burger Chef, you've gotta help him.

6. BURGER CHEF: Quickly Jeff, my Funburger. That'll make him happy.

7. JEFF: Funburger, yeah. That'll cheer him up.

8. (BURGER CHEF LAUGHS) BURGERRILLA: Oh, there's a smile on the wrapper. Wowee!

9. This is fun. F-U-R. Fun. (JEFF LAUGHS)

10. WOMAN: Burgerrilla, all is forgiven. What'd you get?

11. BURGERRILLA: A very happy surprise.

12. BURGER CHEF: That's because Funburgers now have new fun prizes. (LAUGHS)

13. Like this spinner top. BOY: Oh, wow! Neat.

14. Or an iron-on picture patch. BOY 2: Terrific.

15. GIRL: I did it. JEFF: Or this puzzling puzzle

16. or a mini flying disk. BOY 3: Alright!

17. BURGER CHEF: The delicious all beef burger comes with a surprise of a prize.

18. In a new box

19. with Funburger funnies.

20. JEFF: Burger Chef, you're incrediburgable! (BURGER CHEF LAUGHS)

A parade of unusual customers added fun to the Burger Chef commercials. In this one, Burgerilla (an obvious spoof on King Kong) is tamed with Burger Chef's Funburger. (By permission of Burger Chef Systems, Inc./Hardee's Food Systems, Inc.)

assist with the Kool-Aid brand handled then, and today, by Grey Advertising in New York.

A few years before, Grey developed Kool-Aid's famous frosted pitcher with the smiling face into a children's character called Pitcherman. Over the years, this idea has become one of the best known and successful children's campaigns in history. I often wish I had had something to do with its origination.

When Pitcherman was first introduced in television commercials he was almost symbolic. He appeared as a giant in a clumsy red pitcher costume who stumbled around and dispensed Kool-Aid to kids who were obviously delighted with him. But he was not a very well defined personality.

We were assigned to create a summer promotion for Kool-Aid. It was a single, isolated project. Part of the promotion we created was an "Adventures of Pitcherman" comic book. In our comic book adventures we made him a superhero. Whenever kids were in dangerously thirsty situations, particularly after some exhausting exercise, Pitcherman came to the rescue bringing ice cold Kool-Aid to quench thirst. This treatment brought him and his story line into the cultural mainstream as a superhero which ultimately gave him a clearer, better defined identity.

Today, Pitcherman continues his adventures and we get to know him better each season. He now moves with greater speed, makes dramatic entrances and exits, and, best of all, he has an animated face which allows him to talk, sing, and express himself. His greatest characteristic is that he is instantly understood, liked, and found amusing by children everywhere and in every language. He is truly one of the best examples of a children's product as personality. Like Barbie, he is an internationally known character.

Many years after the first exposure to Pitcherman, I left Los Angeles to work for Ogilvy & Mather in an international capacity. One of my assignments was looking after General Foods brands in 24 different countries. Kool-Aid was an Ogilvy brand in many of them. For children's advertising in those countries, we continued to use Grey's Pitcherman formula, merely changing American kids' environments to a soccer match in Colombia, a baseball game in Venezuela and Mexico, a small neighborhood circus in Brazil, and roller skating in the park in France. I even wrote some Pitcherman commercials that were translated into Spanish and Portuguese. In the advertising agency world, it was a perfect example of "a good idea doesn't care who has it."

1. (SFX: TIRES SCREECH)

2. (MUSIC UNDER) SINGERS: Kids play a lot, more than any-one.

3. Kids get hot, more than any-one.

4. KIDS SHOUT: Hey, Kool-Aid!

5. (SFX: RUMBLE)

6. (SFX: CRASH) SINGERS: Kool-Aid is for a kid's

7. big thirst.

8. (SFX)

9. Kids are having fun,

10. more than anyone.

11. Yeah, yeah, yeah...

12. Kids are on the run more than anyone. Ooh!

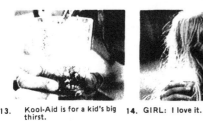

13. Kool-Aid is for a kid's big thirst.

14. GIRL: I love it.

15. ANNCR: (VO) Kool-Aid Brand Soft Drink Mix.

16. SINGERS: Kool-Aid is for a kid's big thirst.

Kool-Aid's Pitcherman is one of the best examples of a children's product as a personality. Pitcherman is treated as a superhero who comes to the rescue in thirsty situations. (Courtesy, General Foods Corp.)

A Collection of Cereal Salesmen

In the early '70s General Foods maintained five different advertising agencies. While Ogilvy was one of the key agencies, the list of GF brands in the United States was rather short. We had Maxwell House coffee, Shake n'Bake, Gaines dog food, and some new product developments. We had nothing from the Post cereal division. When we asked if we were in line to get a cereal brand in the near future, GF management was very cool to the idea. They informed us that we could take on a competitive company's cereals if we wished. We presented to Ralston and won an assignment to introduce a new children's cereal called Cookie Crisp. Once again, the creative chore was given to Los Angeles and tackled by Russ Alben's seasoned kid's advertising group.

The cereal looked like miniature cookies which Ralston had already determined had great appeal to children. After testing eight different creative approaches in very rough television commercial form, the plan preferred most by children was an animated magician named Cookie Jarvis. He immediately differentiated the cereal from the other animated cereal salesmen much as Tony the Tiger, Cap'n Crunch, Sugar Bear, and Fred Flintstone. The new cereal brand suddenly had its own relevant and memorable personality.

Just at its development point, when we and Ralston were rejoicing in our unprecedented high test scores, there was a re-organization in General Foods' marketing management. Jack Keenan, an executive we had worked with on Kool-Aid projects, was put in charge of cereals. When he heard we were working for Ralston, a major competitor, he called time-out. He did not want a group he considered a GF secret weapon working for the competition. We were asked to resign Ralston immediately in exchange for two General Foods cereals, Super Sugar Crisp and Pebbles. Ralston wasn't very happy with us, but they had a badly needed new entry in the children's cereal category, one that gets them a respectable share of the market to this day.

The subsequent work for the two General Foods brands has never been distinguished for its originality. There was no opportunity to create a new product positioning or new product personalities. The successive product managers at General Foods were never able to clearly define Sugar Bear as a product spokesman. He was first introduced in television programming with Sterling Holloway's voice. Later, he changed into a rather laid-back kind of a guy with a voice that sounded a bit like Bing Crosby's. He is neither funny nor heroic so children cannot easily identify with him. He was merely a television spokesman who, after many years of exposure,

1. WITCH: Heh, heh,

2. I feel really mean this morning.

3. BOY: That witch is turning everybody

4. into toads.

5. GIRL: Look, it's Super Sugar Bear.

6. (SFX: LIGHTNING) SUPER SUGAR BEAR: It'll take Super Sugar to sweeten up that old witch.

7. My cereal starts out like this.

8. (SFX) But when Super Sugar is added,

9. (SFX) it turns into Super Sugar Crisp

10. and that's

11. sweet to eat.

12. WITCH: What was I being so mean about?

13. GIRL: Don't know, you're a pretty sweet witch.

14. SUPER SUGAR CRISP: Start your balanced breakfast with Post Super Sugar Crisp cereal. Super Sugar makes it...

15. (SFX)

16. BOY: Sweet to eat!

Sugar Bear is the product spokesman for Post Super Sugar Crisp cereal. As a superhero he's a laid-back kind of guy with a voice that sounds like Bing Crosby's. (Courtesy, General Foods Corp.)

became associated with Super Sugar Crisp. The spokesmen for the other brand, Pebbles, were Fred Flintstone and his pal Barney. They are Hanna-Barbera's licensed characters already known to the audience through their popular television show. In addition, the story line for Pebbles commercials is equally well-known. Fred and Barney are always trying to get the cereal away from one another. They are chasing each other to this day.

Product Personalities Also Sell Toothpaste

Toothpaste has always been one of the most competitive product categories. More new brands fail than succeed. Traditionally the positionings were simple. A toothpaste brand was either a teeth whitener, a breath freshener, or a cavity fighter. There were no new positionings.

When Ogilvy introduced Aim for Lever, it was a whole new idea. It was a gel that was a cavity fighting gel because of its fluoride content; it was a breath freshener; and it tasted good. In fact, it tasted so good that kids loved it and consequently were likely to brush more. That was the introductory campaign and it was enormously successful, taking share points from all other brands including the leader, Procter & Gambles's Crest.

Aim's point about its good taste appealing to kids led Lever and Ogilvy to conclude that they could get kids to ask for the brand if they advertised directly to them. A team in New York started developing various approaches to advertise Aim to kids. Five different treatments were to be chosen for testing.

Procter & Gamble then did something totally out of character with their standard operating procedure. Instead of putting a new advertising approach into a market test where its success would be measured, by them and their competitors, they suddenly came forth with a children's advertising campaign for Crest. It opened nationally with a bang on Saturday morning network television.

Procter & Gamble had seldom advertised any of its products to children. This expertise did not appear to be in their formidable arsenal of advertising tactics; yet, their campaign for Crest toothpaste was right on the money. They invented a team of animated space commandos who were locked in battle with Cavity Monsters. Crest commando teams were superheroes engaged in 30-second adventures against the forces of evil. Anyone who understood anything about kids advertising instantly knew that this positioning didn't need any testing.

58

1. (MUSIC UNDER)
BARNEY: One, and a two,
oh, what I wouldn't do to
get Cocoa Pebbles

2. from you know who.

3. Time for the Pebbles

4. twenty-second work out

5. BARNEY: (ON VIDEO)
Let's work those arms. Five,
six, seven, eight.

6. Hey Fred, you're just looking
great.

7. FRED: Thanks.

8. BARNEY: Let's work that
stomach. Umm,
cocoaliscious.

9. BARNEY: (ON VIDEO)
Now grab a partner for a
little leg work.

10. FRED: Oh Barn...Barney,
my Pebbles.

11. BARNEY: Let's work those
legs.

12. FRED: Post Cocoa and
Fruity Pebbles cereal. Part
of this nutritious breakfast.
Yabba-dabba-delicious.

Post Pebbles cereal uses Fred Flintstone and his pal Barney as their television spokesmen. Both are licensed characters from Hanna-Barbera's Flintstone television series. Fred and Barney are always trying to get the cereal away from each other. (Copyright 1986 Hanna-Barbera Productions, Inc. All rights reserved.)

By the time Lever and Ogilvy finally got through a ponderous testing procedure with an appealing advertising solution, P&G had already captured the children's brand preference.

THE CARTOON BECOMES KING

Television programming for children has come a long way since 1955. In the earlier years, cartoons were purchased from motion picture over-stocks. Properties such as "Krazy Kat," "Kiko the Kangaroo," "Oswald the Rabbit," and "Casper the Friendly Ghost" all appeared on television by 1953. During those same years, 168 old Popeye cartoons were sold to television, and CBS bought all 1,100 of Paul Terry's "Terrytoons" in 1955. The stations put in as large a supply of them as they could handle and the networks opened early Saturday mornings with them and filled in with them when movies ran short. All of these old theatrical shorts ran in hundreds of local shows hosted by sheriffs, locomotive engineers, sea captains, space commanders, and neighborhood policemen. Television was a repository for old animation material, and until it became economically viable, it did not encourage the production of anything new in cartoon form. The kind of full animation which was done by the major studios for theatrical release was simply unaffordable for television.

Producers started experimenting with new techniques using fewer drawings. UPA, the studio that produced "Gerald McBoing Boing" and "Mr. Magoo" became one of the first pioneers. They proved that a story could be told using fewer drawings and by using a variety of angles, cuts, and camera moves to achieve a sense of motion. They surprised the animation industry when they won an Oscar in 1950 for "Gerald McBoing Boing."

Similar production methods were translated to television in 1950 by a young San Francisco animator named Jay Ward. Long before Ward created Rocky and Bullwinkle, he brought forth the first cartoon character made for television, a creature named Crusader Rabbit. Crusader Rabbit appeared in five-minute cartoons with his companion, Rags the Tiger, and they were immediately popular with the stations because of their extremely low cost. Ward made 19 of these cartoons for $1500 apiece.

The cartoon form on television is seldom credited to UPA or Jay Ward. It received its real boost from Bill Hanna and Joe Barbera who had created "Tom and Jerry" at MGM. In Gary H. Grossman's fine history of children's television programming entitled *Saturday Morning TV,* Joe Bar-

1. ANNCR: Day after day, Toothopolis stands behind its beautiful wall of teeth, ever vulnerable to...

2. (MUSIC) ...the cavity creeps. CREEP: We climb tooth. Make hole. (SFX)

3. MAN: The cavity creeps.

4. I'll call the Crest team. (SFX)

5. WOMAN: The siren. The cavity creeps must be near our beloved wall of teeth. MAN: Yes, at the upper back molar.

6. MAN: Hurry into the Crest-mobile.

7. SIREN: Crest, Crest, Crest... MAN: Help us, protect us.

8. CREEP: This good spot for big hole.

9. MAN: We must fight the cavity creeps with our fluoride.

10. WOMAN: Take this, cavity creeps. CREEPS: Crest! Uuuggghhh.

11. PEOPLE: Yeah! Toothopolis is saved.

12. MAN: The cavity creeps are a constant threat to every Toothopolis. WOMAN: So you must fight with us.

13. MAN: Have regular checkups.

14. WOMAN: Watch treats. MAN: And brush after every meal with

15. C-R-E-S-T.

Procter & Gamble's Crest Commando teams are superheroes engaged in battle with Cavity monsters, forces of evil. A 30-second commercial becomes an adventure. (Courtesy, Procter & Gamble)

bera is quoted, "When we went into television with 'Ruff and Ready' in 1957, there was practically no original animation produced for the medium. We had to help test new methods of animating for television. Television didn't have the money; it also didn't have the time."

Barbera goes on to explain that he and his partner used to produce five or six "Tom & Jerry" cartoons a year at MGM for about $40,000 each. In 1957 television paid them about $2,700 for a five-minute cartoon and it had to be made in two weeks. Hanna-Barbera's early experiment with "Ruff and Ready" ushered in a bevy of new animation companies who were only too anxious to use the limited animation techniques for television programming. In fact, television's requirement for these new slapdash shows turned the program creators into mass production houses overnight. Norm Prescott and Lou Scheimer started Filmation; Walter Lantz, who created "Woody Woodpecker," revamped Woody for television; Dave De Patie and Fritz Freleng, who gave us "The Pink Panther" started creating for television; and the networks were suddenly able to fill their Saturday morning time slots with two to three hours of new cartoons back to back. They simply bought film by the pound, created a whole new category of television, and sold it to advertisers at very substantial profits.

The advent of affordable limited animation cartoon shows had another consequence. These shows, which became the new form of almost all children's television, brought the curtain down on live personalities for children. Children's shows featuring such well-known television personalities as Burr Tilstrom, Uncle Johnny Coons, Soupy Sales, Shari Lewis, and Pinky Lee simply went out of fashion. Of those early children's stars, only "Captain Kangaroo" and "Mr. Rogers" remain.

Children's programming, once considered an inconvenience that didn't bring in much money by broadcasters, had suddenly become a lucrative business. There were big bucks to be made on Saturday morning. Barbie and the army of imitators that followed, plus Chatty Cathy, Ken, Tiny Tears, G.I. Joe, Hot Wheels, and the avalanche of cereals, soft drinks, candy, and gum had all irreversibly changed children's television.

As the network coffers seemed to overflow with advertising receipts and the number of cartoon shows abounded, the quality of Saturday morning programs seemed to deteriorate.

Enter Fred Silverman

By 1965, Saturday morning had become, in the critics' and creators' minds, a garbage pile. None of the top executives at the networks wanted to touch, change, or improve its quality. None, that is, but one ambitious

Bill Cosby's "Fat Albert" show from Filmation is one of the few Saturday morning shows that has lasted more than 15 years. It was loved in 1972 and is still loved today. (Copyright 1972 William H. Cosby, Jr. Filmation Associates.)

26-year old executive at CBS named Fred Silverman. Almost single-handedly he brought about dramatic changes in children's television. He was the first network executive to take cartoons seriously and he decided to make Saturday morning more important by treating it as competitively as nighttime.

Silverman overhauled the CBS schedule. He introduced "The New Adventures of Superman" and moved CBS from third place into first. He generated new production ideas, looked seriously at scripts and storyboards, and inspired the creators to produce a new wave of original cartoons. While we had been buying network television for Mattel since 1955, Silverman was the first executive who wanted to talk to us at length and in detail about new programming ideas. Long evenings in New York restaurants and bars were spent by grown men discussing crime-busting dogs, crazy gorillas, and flying mice. It was recognized that Silverman understood how to reach children in droves and advertisers watched his every move—so did the competition, and Saturday morning television not only improved, but became a mature and profitable business.

For advertisers such as Mattel, General Foods, General Mills, Ralston, Quaker, Ideal, Hasbro, Coleco, Kenner, Mars M&M's, and Hershey's, children's television on Saturday morning became the lifeblood of their advertising. None of these companies could afford to stay out of it. The

"The Archie Show" was number one on Saturday morning television ten years ago, but would be hopelessly out-of-date for kids today. Styles of music and dress have changed dramatically.
(Copyright 1977 The Archie Company)

shares of their brands depended upon it. Betting on the winning cartoons of the season became as deadly serious and competitive as any other tactic affecting the sales of their products.

The networks, in their continued race to be the ratings leader on Saturday morning and consequently command the highest advertising rates, have, since Fred Silverman's time, invested more and more production dollars into Saturday morning television. Animated half-hours that could be bought for less than $50,000 in the late '50s have accelerated today beyond $200,000. Networks once bought 26 half hours on original contracts, but now they are reluctant to take risks on new shows and order only 10, 13, or 17 episodes. They try new shows like dipping their toes in cold water, and if ratings fail, they quickly find substitutions. Changes in Saturday morning line-ups are almost as frequent as in prime time. The game is played on ratings and the children's audience has become just as fickle and jaded as the adult viewing audience. They are extremely selective about what they want to watch and even a hit show, in recent years, doesn't last beyond a few seasons. For example, with the exception of Bill Cosby's "Fat Albert" none of the hit Saturday morning children's shows of 15 years ago such as "The Archie Show," "The Beatles," "The Jackson Five," or "Josie and the Pussycats" would even be recognized by today's kids.

MORE CHILDREN'S TELEVISION THAN EVER BEFORE

Beyond the competition between the three networks to capture the largest share of the children's audience, recent years have seen a revival in the syndication of children's shows. While critics and consumerist groups are complaining there is nothing on television for children to watch except the same old Saturday morning cartoons, the individual television stations have found it more and more to their interest to play children's programming all during the week (in the mornings and in the late afternoons). Consequently, there is more children's television now than at any other time in the history of the medium.

Excluding the three Saturday morning networks' two-and-a-half-hour time blocks, and excluding cable television which is playing more and more children's television, and excluding public television which is still playing shows such as "Sesame Street," "The Electric Company," and "3-2-1 Contact," there are currently 42 different animated half-hour series in syndication for children. In addition there are five enormous cartoon libraries such as "Bugs Bunny," "Tom and Jerry," and "Woody Woodpecker" whose episodes number well in the hundreds. Also in syndication are eight live-action series such as "Muppets" and "The Littlest Hobo" and the old "Superman." Also announced and coming into syndication are 20 more children's half-hour shows, almost all projecting 65 episodes per series.

So much children's television is produced today that industry sources predict a glut of animated half-hour programs. Some even foresee at least one of the networks, faced with eroding audience shares and high production costs, getting out of Saturday morning children's television entirely.

From the mid-'40s when all children had on television was "Howdy Doody" and "Kukla, Fran and Ollie," it is astonishing how much children's television has grown. We've virtually gone from too little to too much. Economics once dictated a scarcity and now economics has created a glutted marketplace.

THE PRODUCT HITS OF TODAY

There is more money invested in children's television today than ever before, which, of course, has been the driving force for so many new shows in so many new forms. Advertisers are recognizing that they must

The world's most famous rabbit, Bugs Bunny, has starred in hundreds of his own animated half-hours in both network and syndication. He is a classic children's character appealing to audiences from several generations. (Copyright Warner Bros. Inc. 1966)

TM Indicates Trademark of Warner Bros. Inc. © 1966

use local syndicated programming as well as network to reach the entire children's audience frequently enough.

The more recent toy hits that followed Barbie, Chatty Cathy, and Hot Wheels, such as Strawberry Shortcake, Cabbage Patch Dolls, Transformers, and Care Bears have all been fueled by massive television expenditures to reach children. Essentially, these products have followed more or less the same patterns as the earlier toy hits. Very few new marketing or advertising techniques have been invented since the late '60s. The children's industry, made by television, was in full blossom by then and the years since have essentially been filled by more of the same except, of course, it's been much, much more.

One might say that children's television in all its aspects had its infancy in the '40s and by the '50s was a boisterous young teenager. In 1955 it became a young adult and the lessons learned over the next 15 years brought it to maturity.

CHAPTER 3

How Television Affects Children

FOR <u>SOME</u> CHILDREN, UNDER <u>SOME</u> CONDITIONS, <u>SOME</u> TELEVISION IS HARMFUL. FOR <u>OTHER</u> CHILDREN UNDER THE SAME CONDITIONS, OR FOR THE SAME CHILDREN UNDER <u>OTHER</u> CONDITIONS, IT MAY BE BENEFICIAL. FOR <u>MOST</u> CHILDREN, UNDER <u>MOST</u> CONDITIONS, <u>MOST</u> TELEVISION IS PROBABLY NEITHER PARTICULARLY HARMFUL NOR PARTICULARLY BENEFICIAL.

W. Schramm, J. Lyle, and E. B. Parker.
Television in the Lives of Our Children
Stanford: Stanford University Press, 1961

CHILDREN HAVE ALWAYS BEEN A SPECIAL AUDIENCE

⌐The popular media have always regarded children as a special audience. Advertisers, who drive and finance the popular media, have always thought to provide something of interest to children, if only to win the approval of their parents.⌐

In the late 1800s, one technique was to offer premium booklets of children's stories for parents to give to their child.

At the turn of the century, as we developed more magazines and newspapers, one could find an occasional ad aimed at young readers in such magazines as *American Boy* or *Open Road*. In addition, this period was also the dawn of newspaper comic strips and comic books. Advertising supported these, too.

Children, as a market, were well defined by the time radio became an important medium in the '30s and '40s. In fact, many of radio's children's programs came from such earlier comic strip characters as "Little Orphan Annie" and "Superman," just as television was to develop some of its early programs for children from radio.

The supporters of children's radio programs were bread companies, cereal companies, and nutritional milk powder such as Ovaltine. Perhaps one of the reasons there was so little objection to children's advertising in those days is that most of the products were considered nutritious. Even though cereal companies and Ovaltine were constantly offering children premiums for a few box tops, mothers did not react negatively because the products seemed wholesome and were good sources of energy for their children.

As television developed during the '50s, the nature of the products changed. Beyond the cereal manufacturers, the television advertisers became the makers of candy, chewing gum, toys, peanut butter, and soft drinks. It was quickly recognized that children had become the primary decision-makers in the purchase of these and many other types of products.

In the 1960s, when advertisers discovered that television advertising to this special children's audience could yield excellent sales results, they began probing for additional information about the child viewer and how to communicate effectively with him and her. Researchers began collecting all the data they could. Media researchers started seriously analyzing children's programming. Statisticians, through the Nielsen ratings, began examining the Saturday morning audience flow and picking apart the age group and sexes for each program. Market researchers began dissecting the data looking for differences in children's behavior in different regions, states, and neighborhoods. They discovered how children spent their time, particularly the number of hours per day spent with television. They began analyzing which products were bought for children in the home. Psychologists started observing how and why children watched television, how much of a force it was, and how children reacted to it. Most importantly, in the marketing world, how they reacted to certain commercials. And of course sociologists, fearing that business was exploiting children through television, started probing the ill effects of television on children, finding for the most part that television violence was creating aggressive behavior and that advertising to children was taking unfair advantage of their inability to understand it.

THE DIFFICULTIES OF RESEARCH WITH CHILDREN

All of the researchers found that getting solid research information from children was difficult and presented its own set of problems. Children do not perceive information like adults; they don't think like adults; and they don't express themselves like adults. Communicating with children is a difficult art, to say the least.

In a landmark article published in the *Journal of Advertising Research* in 1965, William White, a professor of psychology at Rutgers University and a consultant and research director for advertising agencies, pointed out the complexities that researchers experience when using children as respondents in advertising research:

1. Children respond very differently between the ages of five and twelve.

2. Children under five are extremely difficult and at times impossible to interview.

3. There are considerable differences in maturity between various eleven- and twelve-year olds which create numerous exceptions to a single point of view concept.

4. Children find abstract concepts hard to understand.

5. Children have trouble extracting the essence from a verbal statement.

6. Children, especially younger ones, cannot separate their reactions to the product advertised and the advertisement itself.

7. Children usually blank out when you ask them "Why?"

8. When a question is hard, there is a negative response. The negative response may be precipitated by a lack of understanding of the question or a reluctance to try and answer it. It's easier to say "no" than to say "I don't know."

9. Because children can remember a television commercial word for word or repeat slogans and jingles, one should not assume they understand the meaning.

10. Children are eager to please, especially when they like the interviewer. They sometimes tell the interviewer what they think the interviewer would like to hear.

It is important to keep these complexities in mind when reading research studies about how children react to television. One must conclude that no conclusive data on the subject exists, only trends, interpretations, assumptions, and hunches—all reliant on imperfect mechanisms for gathering the original data.

Despite the hundreds of millions of dollars spent every year to beam television messages to children, and despite the number of advertisers, advertising agencies, and research firms specializing in children's studies such as Child Research in New York, Judith Langer in New York City, the

Gene Reilly Group in Connecticut, and Cole-Green in California, and the great extent of research by academics on the subject, every hard and fast conclusion drawn by any researcher must be questioned seriously regarding its assumptions and its validity. The entire state of the art of research with children, even after 20 years of probing, is still formative.

Perhaps the most significant work done on the reactions of children to television has been done by Scott Ward, a professor of Business Administration at Harvard University. In the early '70s, Ward published a series of articles and studies in the *Harvard Business Review* and other publications. He also led a massive research study with the Gene Reilly Group in Connecticut. While I am suggesting that no one study or article should be relied upon as gospel, if one studies Ward's work and the thousands of other articles and reports on this subject done by academic researchers and industry, one must glean some simple concepts that should guide us rather than confuse us in communicating with children on television.

DESPITE THE DIFFICULTIES IN READING RESEARCH, HERE'S WHAT WE KNOW

Television and television advertising obviously influence children. If they did not, there would be no children's television today. There has been enough study of the children's market over the past 40 years to tell us that children:

- directly buy products,
- influence the purchase of products,
- influence the purchase of particular brands of products, and
- indirectly influence the purchase of products and brands.
  Their parents just seem to know what they want.

All of the above data have always been so, even before television. However, being the dominant medium it has become, television has drawn greater attention from the children's audience than ever before.

In the case of a children's audience, the process of influence and purchase operates differently than it does with adults. Television advertising often creates an interaction with parents. It's an interaction that's occurring regardless because mothers are inclined to teach consumer orientation to products, prices, and needs. Most likely, parents are trying to get a quality product message across early because they don't want their child to be a frivolous buyer.

CHILDREN'S INFLUENCES VARY WITH PRODUCT CATEGORIES AND AGE

The influence of children is not equal for every product category that interests them. For example, children are far more influential in the purchase of toys, candy, and gum than they are on toothpaste, shampoo, and soap, yet they use all of those products frequently.

The child's age is also a factor in measuring the strength of his or her influence on purchases. As children grow older they have more say about what is bought. Let's take cereals, for example, since it is probably the largest product category that uses children's television to tell its product story. Up to seven years old, children peacefully acquiesce to parental decisions on which to buy. It is understood in the dynamics between parents and child that "Mom and Dad know." From eight to ten, children become extremely articulate and voice their preferences. From 13 to 15, they start behaving like adults.

CHILDREN DO NOT REACT TO TELEVISION ALONE

Children do not react to television in a vacuum. There are two very important information streams that influence how children feel about products:

1. what Mom and Dad say about the product,
2. what he feels he knows about the product from TV, friends, and other sources.

The products the child feels are for him and which he consumes frequently like toys, candy, gum, and snacks are the ones he feels he knows the most about and he relies on what he knows first. For most other products, he relies more heavily on parental judgement.

There is a popular assumption among consumerists that advertising to children via television is a sure-fire path to selling a product. Nothing could be further from the truth, especially in product categories that are comestible. Parents play a key role in buying decisions as they do in the complete socialization of their child as a consumer. Parents must be given a reason to buy as well as children.

If kids are told that a product is fun to eat and tastes good (the two most important food attributes for children), and the television message communicates the story well, chances are children will want and ask for the product. Parents must also be told about the product, but in another way. They want to know why it's good for kids.

When both parties know about the product, a dialogue takes place. These product dialogues and the interaction of kids and Mom occur frequently. If parents believe the product is harmless or good for their children, they usually yield to a child's requests.

As children get older their level of consumer socialization becomes more evident. They become more independent. This clearly arises in their choices of clothes and shoes, particularly sneakers. As they get older and pass the preschool stage they become more involved in the purchase of cold cereals, toys, comic books, soft drinks, and sports equipment.

A two-edged sword exists that television advertisers, especially of new products, must consider when children ask for a product. The mother's opinion of its value suddenly becomes an important and noticeable consideration. If she buys the product and it fails to deliver, she is more likely to say "I'll never buy that again." The fastest way to kill a poor product for children is to advertise it on television.

THE STORE AS CLASSROOM

Children make frequent visits to grocery stores and supermarkets with their parents—the younger the child, the more frequent the visits.

The next time you're in a supermarket, wheel your shopping cart in back of a parent with a child. You will witness a dialogue on various products. You will hear a lot of nos and discussions of costs with the child. In this situation, the store functions as a classroom. The parents teach and the child learns. Parents know they must deal with requests to buy and become quickly attuned to this exercise.

Advertisers, who are acutely aware of the dynamics taking place in the store between mother and child, take special pains with their point of purchase displays and with their packaging. They recognize the need to put real information on the package to reassure mothers of quality.

WHAT HAPPENS IN FRONT OF THE TELEVISION SET

Families frequently watch television together. Commercials often evoke comments from children. If the commercial is one a child has seen before and likes, he will ask everyone in the room to be sure and "watch this one, it's a good one." If it's a commercial he doesn't like, he may react and say "it's phoney" or "dumb." Sometimes commercials prompt a request for a product, giving parents an opportunity to learn the child's favorites. There is no better way for parents to learn what influence television has on their children. If it educates, expands their horizons, and builds their awareness of the worlds, its effect is positive. If the material is overly violent, horrifying, or sexual, it is probably having a negative effect.

PARENTAL WORRIES ABOUT CHILDREN'S REACTIONS TO TELEVISION

Surveys indicate that most mothers worry about too many commercials, too much television watching, the poor content of television, and the insufficient number of good shows for children. Because survey after survey points out these concerns, one wonders why more household rules about television don't exist. It appears that few parents enforce rules about television watching very strictly.

TELEVISION IS A FAVORITE ACTIVITY FOR CHILDREN

In Scott Ward's extensive study of children's television viewing habits, children indicate their favorite activity is "playing with friends" or "going to the movies." After those, "watching TV" becomes the favorite. Since friends aren't always available nor are the movies, television becomes the activity. Situation comedies and adventures rate as favorites. Cartoon shows are also popular. Cartoon shows do not rank highest because they are usually aired at times when children are traditionally expected to watch TV; however, more children are watching at prime time—when sitcoms and adventure shows are being aired—than any other time of the day. Cartoon shows seldom play during prime time.

Children like commercials more than their parents do. Parents are not entirely negative. A good many believe that commercials are a fair price to pay for entertainment, but children find high entertainment value in commercials and enjoy learning about products, even though they don't believe all the commercials. The youngest ones (six-seven) believe and enjoy commercials the most. Older children become increasingly cynical, pointing out that commercials "are trying to make people buy things."

Is It Fair to Advertise to Children?

Because it is now obvious that children like television commercials and react to them by making product requests, whether or not it is ethical to advertise to them has become a hotly debated issue. Consumerist groups have exerted considerable pressure to ban television advertising to children altogether. Because children react favorably to television, some adults assume they are malleable, innocent, and unable to cope with advertising.

As research points out, children do influence purchases. But only after an interaction with their parents. In addition, research indicates that they become more cynical and selective as they grow older and that they discriminate at four or five years old.

Marketers must appeal to kids because advertising creates an interaction between parents and children that affects the buying process. Since they influence part of the buying process, they must be reached in a way they understand—which differs from the way advertisers reach their parents. Research indicates that children have different levels of fantasy and imagination. They have different tastes, different interests, and different social needs; consequently, if advertising is to communicate with this audience effectively, it must be carefully considered in light of these differences. The appeal to children through television is a recognition of their individuality and rightful interest in the products they use. These appeals also recognize that children's decisions aren't made alone. Those who would ban advertising to children would also deny children the opportunity to participate in family decision making. While the requests and nagging for particular products may be irritating to parents, it is a healthy process that helps build the child's idea of himself. A child is eventually going to decide what he or she eats and plays with and he or she could participate with misinformation or no information at all.

Advertising to children has certain benefits for the child and family. It helps the child recognize diversity in choice. He or she soon learns the ability to reject. This process of selection motivates makers of children's products to make products that best fit children's needs and interests.

Advertising to children sets up a process in which a child has an opportunity to choose for him- or herself. There is dialogue with an adult, but the product is not solely interpreted by the adult. The child has a point of view, and if he or she ends up not liking the product, he or she must accept the responsibility for its purchase. In this way, the child develops more careful buying habits and keeps the family from wasting money.

The greatest advertising controversy exists around products eaten for breakfast, specifically sugar-sweetened cereals. Cereal advertising to children must now point out that cereal is only part of a complete breakfast. As a result, breakfast eating among children is up, the incidence of eating complete breakfasts is up, and whether complete or incomplete, either is better than no breakfast at all—which used to be reasonably common.

DOES TELEVISION ADVERTISING RAISE PRICES?

Many people claim that the cost of TV advertising forces companies to sell higher-priced goods to children; upon examination, however, quite the contrary is true. Advertising actually reduces prices. Toy items advertised on television are heavily discounted, so are candies, cereals, and snacks. The argument disputing higher prices for television advertised toys is particularly well stated in a letter that Bernie Loomis, as head of all of General Mills' toy companies, sent to Michael Pertschuk, then Chairman of the Federal Trade Commission, in 1977. Some excerpts from the letter follow:

> The Toy Manufacturer's Association fact book expresses a number of important reasons why television advertising of toys to children is an appropriate and responsible activity.
>
> My purpose is to give substance to just *one* of the reasons why television advertising to children is proper and valuable—and that reason is the significant economic benefit to the consumer.
>
> Attached to this letter are a few examples to support this contention. Attachment #1 is page 445 of the current J.C. Penney Christmas 1977 catalog. None of the items on this page are television advertised. They are attractively presented and, although they are not made by us, I am most certain that the cost price of each of the items is roughly one-half of the retail selling price, representing fair value and normal retailing practice to the consumer.
>
> Compare this page to attachment #2, page 449 of the same catalog—a page featuring television advertised items. Beautiful Baby Alive is offered for $11.47. J.C. Penney pays us $9.90. The 3-in-1 Nursery Center is offered at $7.77. J.C. Penney pays us $5.95. The Stroller-Rocker is offered at $9.77. J.C. Penney pays us $8.40. Baby Heartbeat is offered at $10.97. J.C. Penney pays us $9.90.

Another even more dramatic example is attachment #3. A K-Mart ad from November 27th. K-Mart is the largest retailer of toys in the United States. Featured in this ad on the page of dolls are three Kenner products—Baby Alive, Baby Heartbeat, and Baby Won't Let Go. They are offered for sale at $9.97 each and K-Mart pays us $9.90 each for these dolls. On the page of toys, four additional Kenner items are shown—the Oscar Goldman, Six Million Dollar Man, Maskatron, and Bionic Woman action figures. All of them are offered at $6.97 each. K-Mart pays us $6.90 each. In the center of the same page, you will note a Chalk Board/Peg Board offered at $15.88. I do not know who the manufacturer is. It is not a television advertised item, but I will state with total confidence that the cost price of the item is in the range of 60% of the retail selling price.

Mr. Pertschuk, I'm prepared to submit, as I'm sure every major toy company is, literally hundreds of such examples of the economic benefit to the consumer of television advertised toys. These items represent well in excess of $1,000,000 of investment on our part and are only economically feasible at our selling prices on the basis of being able to project sales in the hundreds of thousands of unit range. Television advertising makes it possible. Without it, Baby Alive wouldn't exist and Baby Alive is now almost five years old, and no product survives for five years in our industry, or even prospers for one year unless it has *fully demonstrated sustained play value to the child.*

The assumption that the end user, the child, is unsophisticated as a consumer has resulted in the death of more than one toy company, Topper Toys being a leading example. Television advertising to children functions as a two-stage rocket. You can achieve effective trade distribution and a certain number of early sales but then it's up to the kids. Unlike their parents, they are vocal and communicative and if they don't enjoy the toy on a sustained basis, they will tell their peers and all of the television advertising in the world won't make a toy without play value economically successful. If they do like it, that same peer communication is capable of creating a demand that outstrips the planned production capacity of any manufacturer. Year after year major toy manufacturers find themselves cutting back the planned advertising because the demand level is literally beyond the supply capability. An even stranger phenomenon takes place that when an item becomes "hot and short," retailers offer it at even lower prices in recognition of the pulling power of the item. It's a sensitive system Mr. Pertschuk, but it works. It delivers economic value to the consumer and play value to the child and it results in the lowest priced toy market in the world.

Baby Alive is a leading seller in many countries throughout the world at prices two and three times higher than in the U.S., where the unique combination of competitive retailing and television advertising of toys works.

When I was a child, the leading producers of toys were Germany and Japan. Today U.S. toys dominate the world market as a direct outgrowth of the merchandising and advertising system that I have attempted to describe above.

ADVERTISING IS A HOLISTIC PROCESS

Too often consumerist groups view advertising to children as exploitation. They see it as isolation, a negative force that influences children to buy things they do not need. What they do not recognize is that advertising itself is a holistic process.

- It forces the retailer to provide a wider variety of products.
- It creates competition so that one or two marketers cannot establish an unshakable position.
- Advertising creates self-policing. Bad products are soon weeded out if they don't deliver. 7
- Advertising and the entire system of marketing products to children forces the marketer to do research and extensive homework.
- The marketer must position the product to suit children's needs and interests. The marketer must test the product with children to assure a proper fit.
- Products must meet stringent economic criteria.
- Advertising must derive from the product and it must be tested to assure the message is clear and that there is an absence of an unintended message.

"Shooting Fish in a Barrel?"

Advertising revenues underwrite children's television. Without entering the subjective argument as to which programs for chidren are of high quality, it should be pointed out to those who complain that we do not have enough children's programming, that advertising has made it possible to have more children's programming today than at any other time in the history of television.

To consumerist groups and politicians who have complained that advertising to children through television is essentially an unfair practice tantamount to "shooting fish in a barrel," I would quickly point out that if it were that simple, all products advertised to children on television would be successful. Quite the opposite is true.

As I indicated elsewhere, the Barbie doll has had countless imitators over the past 25 years. Most had impressive television budgets and sold for less at retail than Barbie. Yet, most of these imitations failed and are no longer on the market.

One might well ask why there are so few new candy bars on the market. Many new ones have been tried. All the contemporary advertising techniques have been used, including licensing the name of a premier athlete on the product as in the case of the Reggie bar named for baseball great, Reggie Jackson. This product had a brief flurry of sales and is currently off the market.

New cereal brands come and go. New candies and gums come and go. So do new drinks, new toys, and new styles in sneakers. All are introduced to children on television and only a few survive beyond a season or two. The losses on unsuccessful products for children are staggering.

What consumerists fail to realize is that the so-called "fish in the barrel" are discriminating consumers, despite their years. They are a fickle, faddish, constantly changing audience.

The Question of Sugar-Sweetened Products

Perhaps the greatest controversy surrounding advertising to children and its ill effects regards nutrition or the absence of it in children's products. The central complaint focuses on the question of sugar and dental health.

Unquestionably, too much sugar is bad for children's teeth, but to place the blame on advertising, or to ban the advertising of sugared products is ludicrous and unnecessary. If candy weren't advertised, would kids eat less candy? If presweetened cereals disappeared entirely, non-sweetened cereals would still require sugar. Perhaps sugar consumption would be reduced from 16 grams per meal to 13 grams per meal—a difference of 40 ounces per year, but there is no evidence that even this change would take place. In fact, there is no proof whatsoever, no link between advertising sugared products and dental health. When the entire matter was brought before the government, as many dental authorities reputed the claims of sugar damage as those who saw the harm in it. It was also established that eating an apple has as much sugar as a bowl of cereal.

Banning television advertising of sugar-sweetened products is clearly not the answer. The ban on television cigarette advertising has not reduced smoking in teenagers. Children do what their families do. If parents regard sugar as acceptable, so do their children. Parents must determine the amount of sugared products their children use.

THE QUESTION OF VIOLENCE

In the earliest days of television no one knew much about how television programs affected children. No one knew that violence as seen in cartoons and live-action programs instilled more aggression in children than they would otherwise have. In recent years, however, a number of in-depth sociological studies have explored this issue. The largest of these studies (six volumes and a summary) was initiated in 1969 and carried out by the U.S. Surgeon General's office. This office concerns itself with national physical and mental health—it's most famous report being the one which linked cigarette smoking to lung cancer, the results of which banned cigarette advertising from television.

As indicated earlier in this chapter, any solid research on child behavior is terribly complicated. The objectives of the research made the process doubly complex because the subject was new and largely uninvestigated. If a child chooses a particularly violent show and then behaves aggressively, did the program promote this behavior? Or did the child pick the show because he was aggressive to begin with?

The Surgeon General's study, the later comments about it by other sociologists and psychologists, and the later independent studies by other scientists all set about investigating three different possibilities (and each of these possibilities has its proponents) regarding the link between television and violence:

1. Television has no significant relationship to aggressive behavior.
2. Television reduces aggressive behavior.
3. Television causes aggressive behavior.

A variation on the third possibility is that both television viewing and aggressive behavior are related not to each other, but to a third variable that mediates between the first two.

The Surgeon General's findings included indications that there just might be a connection between television violence and aggressive behavior, although the relationships were far from clear. If you are looking for a sharper and more definitive answer to this question, there is none. Opinions vary with each possibility. Nevertheless, everyone who was at the hearings, including representatives from all three television networks, concluded there was cause for concern and encouraged more detailed study—research that scientists call longitudinal studies that would measure a definite group of people over a long period of time. Studies of this type and further analyses of the data from these studies are still being conducted today.

The networks, much to their credit, did not treat this problem as a question mark. They reacted by rejecting their old libraries of cartoon series that were considered too violent and from then on encouraged their cartoon program suppliers to produce stories with toned down violent material. In addition, some advertisers started to use their buying power to veto programs that were violent or not in the public interest.

One of the other results stimulated by the Surgeon General's report was research on a corollary question: If television violence can induce aggressive behavior, can pro-social programming stimulate positive behavior? By 1975 this question became one of the most important questions for researchers in the field. The literature on the subject today confirms that children learn from pro-social messages included in programs designed to impart such messages. The networks responded to this by asking their cartoon producers to include pro-social messages in their shows and by creating pro-social shorts that are broadcast between shows on Saturday mornings.

1. (MUSIC UNDER) KERMIT THE FROG: Don't forget to put your skates away, Animal.

2. ANIMAL: Okay.

3. (MUMBLES) Wow!

4. KERMIT AND ROWLF: Huh?

5. (SFX: SKATES)

6. MISS PIGGY: Ooh.

7. (SFX: SCREECH)

8. (SFX: SKATES)

9. (SFX: CRASH)

10. ANIMAL: Oh.
KERMIT THE FROG: Thanks, Animal.
ANIMAL: Welcome.

11. (LAUGHS)

12. ROWLF: Hey, it's almost 10 o'clock.

13. SCOOTER: Mammy's supposed to take us to the art museum today.

14. SKEETER: I'll go remind her.

15. Whoa!

16. (SFX: THUMP)

17. (CRIES) KERMIT THE FROG: Are you okay, Skeeter?

18. SKEETER: I don't think so. I hurt my ankle.

19. MAMMY: What was that shout?

20. SKEETER: I tripped on a roller skate, Mammy.

The networks have asked their cartoon producers to include pro-social messages in their shows. The example shown here is from Jim Henson's "Muppet Babies" currently airing on CBS on Saturday mornings. The example lets children know the dangerous consequences of leaving a roller skate out where someone can stumble on it. (1985 Henson Associates, Inc. Reprinted by permission.)

Other Ill Effects of Television on Children

In recent years, the effects of television on children has become a popular subject for academic researchers. Their probings have gone far beyond the question of violence and today a vast body of serious literature on this subject exists. Some of the research findings that take up this issue are:

1. Television is a passive medium; children passively absorb the information they get from television—violence, sex, commercials, etc.
2. Television viewing decreases creativity in children.
3. Television viewing is an addictive behavior.

At least one of these researchers, Kathy Pezdek, an Associate Professor of Psychology at the Claremont Graduate School, has indicated that these findings are all myths and has refuted these myths in an article entitled "Is Watching TV Passive, Uncreative or Addictive? Debunking Some Myths," published in *Television & Families,* Vol. 8/Number 2 in 1985. Pezdek herself is a research psychologist who has devoted her career to the cognitive processing of television.

Her refutation of the passive watching claim quotes from other researchers as well and it points out that children are not overwhelmed by television and they seldom watch without some other activity in the room. They do not simply stare at television like "couch potatoes." They look at television back and forth depending upon program content. Her position is that television is an active process in many ways similar to reading. One study indicates that when children have alternate activities in the room, they only look at television half of the time. One could conclude that the time children spend watching television is not spent watching television and that children are actively and selectively gathering information while watching television.

As for television stifling creativity in children, there is also no definitive literature proving this point. Pezdek and M.A. Runco tested the common belief that while radio used to stimulate creativity, visual stories on television no longer left any room for the imagination. The concept was tested with third-graders and sixth-graders with a story presented on both television and radio. The results were clear; television and radio did not differentially stimulate children's creative thinking.

Television has been called a "plug-in drug" and consequently, an addiction. Some children have, in the research, said, "It makes me watch it, I can't help it." The term "addictive" is pure hyperbole. Even people who have said they feel that television is addictive admit that they do not need increasingly larger doses to satisfy their need for television, that they have little or no control over the use of television, and that they do not make substantial sacrifices in order to maintain high levels of television consumption.

It is apparent that television for children is just an easy-to-initiate activity that becomes habitual because it's the easiest thing to do. However, when children spend four to eight hours a day watching television, a serious problem exists at home. But this is a problem in the family, not in the television.

CAN TELEVISION BE BLAMED FOR ALL THE PROBLEMS?

It is fairly common to blame television for all sorts of problems with today's children. Television gets the blame for poor reading scores, poor school performance, aggressive behavior, family problems, and poor mental health. In reality, the reasons for much of the troubling social behavior in children and younger generations are far more profound than television. Until recent years most people lived in a rather well-established social order that had great stability. A long-standing ethical fabric held things together. Children and young people knew what was expected of them, grew up, and took their places in society. Today, particularly in highly industrialized societies, old values are eroding. The knowledge of alternative life-styles, the high degree of mobility, the growth of cities, and a rising level of permissiveness, promiscuity, crime, and divorce have placed the institutions that stabilized society—the family, the church, the community, and the state—all on very shaky ground. The traditional values that held things together are slowly slipping away.

The difficulties facing children in the United States are compounded by a bombardment of media. We not only have three networks, but more television stations than ever before. We have new media delivery systems with over 9,000 cable stations and a fast-growing use of VCRs in the home. With so much information coming at children from all directions, it is increasingly difficult for young people to sort things out and make value judgements.

Just because television has the capacity to educate and enrich children's lives, it cannot be faulted for failing to do so in all cases. These are goals that continue to challenge broadcasters who have had notable successes along with failures and disappointments. They, like the parents, schools, and churches that have been trying to communicate with children for centuries, are trying to improve on what is obviously a very difficult art.

CHAPTER 4

How to Communicate with Children on Television

CHILDREN AGED TWO TO 11 ARE EXPOSED ON AVERAGE TO 20,000 COMMERCIALS a year. That's somewhere between 150 and 200 hours of pure commerial messages—either in 30-second or 60-second doses.

Most of those messages are about cereals, toys, non-carbonated beverages, snacks, candy, and chewing gum. The manufacturers of these products and others primarily consumed by children invest more than $500 million a year trying to tell children about the virtues of their particular brands. Children are being courted and cultivated for their buying power.

Generally, there is not a great deal of differentiation between brands within a given category. Since most products within a given category tend to be very much alike in their purpose, look, flavor, texture, and use, advertisers try to make their products more appealing or different by adding a fun element, often borrowing interest from some other reference within the child's culture. Eventually, children begin to see through this technique. The sheer accumulation of television commercials makes children cynical.

THEY DON'T BELIEVE EVERYTHING THEY'RE TOLD ON TELEVISION

Younger children, aged five to six, tend to be greater believers of commercial messages, but these children rely more on parental decisions anyhow; however, by the time a child is 11 or 12 he or she has decided much of the advertising he or she sees is a sham. The drop in attention span is considerable—so is interest in children's television. The middle group, children seven to nine, like commercials more and pay more attention. They are also heavier watchers of television.

It isn't easy to communicate with children in any of the age groups. It's certainly not as easy as television's critics would have you believe. Adults look at children's television commercials through their own eyes, intelligence, and experience and suppose that children are so innocent and gullible that they will swallow the whole proposition before them. This is hardly the case. Ask any articulate child some questions in-depth about almost any given commercial. You'll be surprised at the reservations and the distrust.

That children are a special audience is true. But the social, educational, and parental caretakers of children are the ones who perceive children as helpless, without understanding that children are perceiving images differently than adults. This attitude of protectionism is rooted in the 19th Century, when children were regarded as property that belonged to parents. All legal, philosophical, and religious precedents sustained this perception of children. Children were, and still are, seen as miniature adults. They are looked upon as empty receptacles that must be filled up with adult ideas and values. What isn't realized is that while these miniature adults are in their first 12 to 15 years of growth, they are usually out of step on an adult staircase.

Children must be viewed as the world's largest minority group. They have their own language, their own level of understanding, and their own view of the adult world. The words and pictures that communicate to adults do not necessarily communicate the same things to children. These different levels, needs, and rights must be respected and nurtured.

CHILDREN ARE NOT ONE MARKET

Children under 12 are not one market; they are three or four segmented markets. Children in these markets are constantly developing and within a 12-year period they progress from infancy to almost the independency of adulthood.

Over this time there is a constant need by the child to change his feelings of weakness and helplessness into competence with people and things. The child strives to reverse his feelings of being small, weak, and incompetent to becoming capable, knowledgeable, and victorious over the challenge of living.

As children pass through their early stages, their rate of mental growth is enormous. A few years makes for very dramatic differences. A five-year old and a 12-year old have less in common than a 20-year old and a 40-year old.

The Preschooler

The one- to five-year olds can't read and rely more on parental decisions. These children are highly stimulated by television and can watch it for hours at a time. They do not take in whole messages, only parts. They are not yet capable of putting the parts together and only retain fragments of any particular message. Their comprehension increases when the visual part of the message is very clearly defined. They also react better to passive, quiet television programming that is organized in short bursts. The attention span of this group is short; they simply cannot follow a long story.

The Six to Nines

The six- to nine-year olds are the most fad conscious. They are the real fans of children's television and make or break the Saturday morning shows or the shows in late afternoon syndication. They are the heaviest watchers of television, the kids who love cartoon shows, the sitcoms, and adventures.

A child coming out of the toddler, preschool, and kindergarten stage is suddenly aware that he or she is no longer a child, but a boy or a girl. Sexual identity has suddenly become an important issue.

Children of this age are most intrigued by speed, power, skill, and beauty. The stories they understand and relate to best are those of the hero and winner. The hero performs a deed, kills an ogre, defeats the bad guys, outwits the villain, or marries the princess or prince.

This group also starts to become involved with friends. The things their friends do, eat, wear, play with, and talk about become a paramount factor in their lives. Peer and fad influence are terribly important.

Certain attitudes and activities come into play:

- Boys are not yet interested in the opposite sex but girls are using male-female relationships as part of their play fantasy.
- Skills such as building, painting, or doing have become part of their lives.

- Possessing and collecting are important. This is the age for the beginning stamp collector and the collector/trader of baseball cards.
- This is the time when learning how things work begins to emerge. There is a fascination with flashlights, radios, and consumer electronics of all sorts.

In short, this is the phase where a child learns to be a consumer of products beyond those he eats and drinks.

The Preteen

The 10- to 12-year olds are a subculture unto themselves. They have their own mannerisms, argot, and point of view. Essentially, they begin to imitate the teenager. They regard themselves as much older than the eight-year old. At this age:

- Fantasies are expressed through real people rather than animals or fairy princesses or superheroes.
- Their appearance and behavior start to become more adult-like. So does their speech.
- They want to be in vogue with teenage fads and fashions.
- Horizons start to turn away from the home. Special bonds develop with their peers. There is a secret sharing of problems and a kind of "double life" begins to form, the one they experience at home and the one they have with their friends.
- Parental influence on dress, hairstyles, and footwear as well as other values begins to diminish.
- Other adult figures enter their lives as heroes—usually from the sports or entertainment world.
- The desire to learn becomes more closely associated with the payoff of a better future.
- They are more interested in winning prizes or contests.

With differences as dramatic as all of the aforementioned, how is it possible to talk to all of them the same way at the same time?

It simply isn't.

As a parent, can you get through to your kids? Visualize the job of the professional communicator who is trying to get through to millions at the same time. Is it any wonder that children's programs and/or commercials appear so simpleminded. The communicator, without a sharp focus on which group he or she is addressing, risks going over the heads of the younger ones or appearing dumb to the older ones. In commercials, where brevity is essential, omissions of certain details appear deliberately dishonest and the inclusion of too many details is both awkward and confusing to the younger part of the group. I am convinced that any critic of children's commercials should try to write one. They would develop a greater understanding of the problem. It is a difficult and perplexing art at best.

Keep It Simple

The younger the child one tries to communicate with through television, the simpler the message must be. The structure of the message must have meaning and pattern—a beginning, a middle, and an end. The sequence must be clear. Changes of scene or color can help add recognition to the sequences.

There should be a clear contrast between what is happening in the foreground and whatever is in the background. Again, color and shape can help the child discriminate. If you have a group of children playing in the foreground, there should be none in the background. Try to clearly establish the person, place, or thing.

The Difficulties of the Art

As children get older, more complex messages can be utilized. The ones over six can correlate parts of a message into a whole in a way younger ones cannot. It is for this group and older that the writer of television commercials can begin to expand and tell more imaginative and complex stories. Some of the most creative and memorable commercials and advertising campaigns, such as those for the Barbie doll, Kool-Aid, Oscar Mayer, and M&M candies, have been designed to reach this group.

Writing commercials for this age group is indeed a difficult and delicate art. The best ones have used fantasy or a certain child-like realism with which children can identify. For the adult writer, finding the idea and just the right tone, striking the right chord of authenticity, can be a difficult creative exercise. I have often likened it to the difficulty a trained and talented artist has in making a drawing that looks like it has been done by a child. I've seen this over and over again and too frequently the art and technique comes off too sophisticated. Anyone who has ever looked at a drawing by a six-year old can spot the difference.

Just as an artist might try such a drawing with his opposite hand to get just the primitive and shaky quality of a child's art, the writer may fall back into his own childhood experience. He will reach back into his own remembrances of childhood experiences, fantasies, language, relation-ships, or quirky situations and then re-create that experience. This way is good, better than most. But it can lead to some traps. A good rule is to ignore maxims from the adult world. Try to separate the child's world from the world as you know it today. And above all, don't try to substitute your own tastes or interests as they are today for a child's.

Don't get trapped in the adult's remembered childhood experience by using just anything you remember. Too many things have changed over the years and you must be mindful of those changes. For example, soap-box derbies, big-little books, marbles, and mumblety-peg are obviously not what they used to be. Today's kids will probably not remember Bill Haley's Comets, Chubby Checker, or even the Supremes. Toy soldiers have been replaced by G.I. Joe, and the characters from *Star Wars* and "He-Man and the Masters of the Universe." Cinderella has lost out to Strawber-ry Shortcake.

How to Position Your Product

As is the case of products for adults, the most important decision an advertiser must make is how to position the children's product.

The marketplace is filled with many brands of cereals, toys, candy bars, cookies, and other products that already have an image with chil-dren. How does your product fit in? What is there about your product that will make it different or more appealing than the brands already in exis-tence.

A simple way of thinking about it in the child's world is for the advertiser to ask himself, *who am I?* Think of all the brands on the market as people or individual personalities. Then ask yourself, *what's different about me?* How will children like my face, my smile, my voice, and the things I say and do? Will they remember me out of the crowd? Perhaps this simplification of the need for correct positioning seen in children's terms is one of the reasons so many children's products identify them-selves with a memorable person or animal.

Novelty is an important factor with children. They like new things and new ideas. When introducing a new product, be sure you communicate the important information about your product that makes it new. How does it taste? What makes it work? What is it made of? After the product has been advertised and on the market a while, you can shift to a concentration on key or salient points of the product. At the beginning, though, the mere fact that the product is new is a positioning of sorts. Concentrate less on the personality of the product; instead, give a lot of information to back up the idea that the product is not something seen before.

Diagnostic research with children is the only way you can determine not only what to say, but how to say it so it will be understood. It will also give you some clues on the positioning.

ESTABLISHING BRAND LOYALTY

A basic rule in positioning a kids' product is to create a unique and distinct image of the product in children's minds. If you do so, and stress the originality of your product, children will, if they like the product after purchase, practice intense brand loyalty and won't easily switch, unless a competitive product comes along and provides obviously greater benefits. They know what they want and what they don't want is a reasonable facsimile. If a girl makes up her mind that she wants a Barbie doll, she won't accept another. When Barbie was first introduced there was no such problem. It was the only fashion doll on the market. Over the past 25 years there have been countless imitators. As a reaction to some of the earliest copycats, we hung a little tag on Barbie's wrist and pointed out to children in the commercials that *only* the one and only original Barbie carried that tag.

New candy bars are difficult to introduce because most kids have already developed a candy hit list. It's a habit we carry over into adult-hood. Usually the list has three or four favorite bars on it. As the mood strikes a child (or an adult), he or she asks for one of the favorite bars. If the absolute favorite isn't available, he or she will try for the second or the third. But how many times have you looked for your favorite bar at the candy or refreshment counter in a movie theater, for example. Chances are if it was not there, rather than get a substitute for one of your favorites, you did without or settled for popcorn.

Kool-Aid is another example of a dominant franchise with children. It is a brand that has almost become synonymous with non-carbonated drinks. The only other brands which sell at all are Hi-C because mothers, not children, perceive it to be higher in nutrients; or Hawaiian Punch because it has some flavors Kool-Aid has not effectively promoted.

A brand that is popular with children takes on a meaning far beyond personal preference. There is peer pressure within the child's world to use the right one—a pressure that doesn't exist to the same degree with adults.

Breaking in or taking the lead away from a popular children's brand, by convincing kids to ask for a substitute, is exceedingly difficult. But it can be done. More likely, however, it must be done with a genuine product innovation than with advertising alone.

Recall the Hot Wheels story. For many years the small die-cast metal cars played with and collected by six- to nine-year old boys were a brand called Match Box. The brand was so strong that the entire category, regardless of maker, was referred to as Match Box-type cars. The brand was so old, so dominant, and so well-respected by the trade, any company would have appeared foolish trying to compete for leadership.

Despite all that, in the early '60s Mattel decided to bring out a line of die-cast metal cars of their own—with two key points of difference. Firstly, Mattel's cars, called "Hot Wheels," could, with the force of gravity alone, run on plastic tracks at phenomenal speeds. Secondly, instead of the classic car designs used by Match Box, "Hot Wheels" had California custom styling. In its introductory year, "Hot Wheels" alone sold in greater volume than the entire category, including Match Box and others, had sold in the year before. The additions made the cars successful.

SOME WAYS TO POSITION CHILDREN'S PRODUCTS

There are several proven ways to position a children's product. One is to create a popular children's personality from the product itself. Television commercials help in doing this. Television commercials made Mattel's Barbie doll a major personality. Barbie, for more than 28 years now, has been the most famous fashion model in the world for children. Strawberry Shortcake, a cute diminutive little doll with a colorful and distinctively strawberry outfit, was positioned in exactly the same way—as a personality. Her name and image were carried on hundreds of different products.

More recently, the same positioning was used for a line of plush, stuffed bears. While the Teddy Bear has been with us almost a century, this

1. (MUSIC UNDER) ANNCR: (VO) Soggies

2. out to sog an innocent break-fast.

3. SOGGY 1: It's breakfast, all right. He, he, he, he.

4. SOGGY 2: Just remember to look out

5. for Cap 'n Crunch.

6. SOGGY 1: Yeah. His cereal's got crunch power

7. to lock taste in so it's tough to sog out.

8. SOGGY 2: Well, I don't see him so...

9. (SFX: SPLASH)

10. ANNCR: (VO) Will breakfast be sogged?

11. CAP 'N CRUNCH: I'll save it with my Cap 'n Crunch Cereal.

12. SOGGY 1: Yipes.

13. CAP 'N CRUNCH: Crunch power locks taste in

14. so it's tough to sog out.

15. He got the point.

16. ANNCR: (VO) Cap 'n Crunch is a crunchy part of this fellow's breakfast. SOGGY 2: Phooey!

Quaker's Cap'N Crunch is a character designed to be both a spokesman and the name of the product itself. As a character he is popularized every time the cereal package is on the table. (By permission of Quaker Oats.)

new line of Care Bears projected human personalities and attributes. Their name and image also appeared on a vast line of children's products, from clothing to toothbrushes.

Curiously, both Strawberry Shortcake and Care Bears came from the same creators. The man primarily responsible for the concept and positioning is Bernie Loomis, an executive who spent many years at Mattel learning his craft. Creating products with personalities, or personalities as product, has become his specialty, and he has been more successful with this technique than any other modern practitioner.

The use of personalities as products is not confined to the world of toys. Cereals use them, too. Tony the Tiger is a popular product personality. He is the spokesman for Kellogg's Frosted Flakes and was developed solely for this use. Other typical examples in cereals are Quaker's Cap'n Crunch and General Mills' Count Chocula and Frankenberry, Trix the Rabbit, Toucan Sam, and Lucky Leprechaun.

While it may seem like a minor distinction, it is important to remember that some characters are designed to be spokesmen while others are the name of the product itself. Quaker's Cap'n Crunch is a good example of the latter. When the name of the character and the name of the product are the same, greater advertising mileage can be gained from the character, and he is popularized every time the package is placed on the table.

Even a non-carbonated drink can be humanized and positioned as a personality. Remember the story of Kool-Aid's Pitcherman. For years the image of Kool-Aid was a smiling face drawn on the outside of a frosty pitcher. Suddenly the pitcher itself came to life (about 10 years ago) and Pitcherman is now depicted in commercials as a superhero who comes dashing and crashing his way to the rescue of thirsty children.

Once a major personality is established, it is important to keep him or her famous. The continuing success of a brand depends on it. Beyond the television commercials that must be kept fresh and interesting from season to season, there are ancillary techniques. Kool-Aid has used promotional comic books containing the further adventures of Pitcherman. The characters are prominently displayed in in-store promotions.

These major personalities, often created solely with television commercials, become licensable characters. They are so popular with children that other manufacturers want to use them for other products. For example, at the peak of Barbie's popularity, she had more than 100 licensees. To this day, at least 40 manufacturers other than Mattel make and market Barbie products. Strawberry Shortcake and Care Bears were conceived more as licensable characters than they were as products themselves. The proliferation of these products in the marketplace became advertising in itself. In a way, their presence in the stores becomes a promotional extension of the television.

Another technique that goes beyond television advertising is the creation and airing of television specials. Both Strawberry Shortcake and Care Bears were half-hour television specials as part of their introduction to the market. This technique has been widely copied and there have been several more specials made and aired for products positioned as personalities, namely G.I. Joe, Herself the Elf, and The Get-Along Gang. The technique has become so common, the animated television special has become almost an essential ingredient in any new product introduction to children. (See chapter five, "The Licensed Character —Today's Hottest Salesman.")

THE PERSONALITY AS SPOKESMAN

Some products are personalities in themselves, for example, Barbie, Strawberry Shortcake, G.I. Joe, and Transformers. Other products use personalities as spokesmen, and, as such, get the rub-off from that spokesman. There is a distinct difference in the two techniques. Obviously, some products cannot be personalities and some can function with or without the personality representing them. For example, Tony the Tiger, who is inextricably connected with Kellogg's Frosted Flakes, is a favorite of both children and adults. The product could exist with or without Tony or another spokesman, but today Tony the Tiger is a well-known character who effectively differentiates Kellogg's Frosted Flakes from the myriad brands of other cereal, and the two effectively exist as one.

Ronald McDonald is a similar sort of character. He is a high-spirited and fun-loving clown who invites children to come to McDonald's. You never see him in the McDonald's commercials aired in the evening.

I've already described the creation of "Burger Chef," an animated, jolly old gent with a sidekick named Jeff, a spirited young teenager, who served up hamburgers, became the television salesmen for Burger Chef as well as the store's identity on posters, tent cards, and packaging. The characters, as kids saw them, were instantly recognizable, lovable, and memorable. They gave these rather ordinary hamburger restaurants their own unique character no one could duplicate. It was obvious from the number of young families with children who started coming to the stores that television advertising had captivated the minds of the children.

POSITIONING BY A UNIQUE CHARACTERISTIC

One of the best and most memorable ways of positioning a product is by taking advantage of some unique physical property the product possesses. For example, if a product is exceptionally large for its category. Or the product may make an unusual sound such as Rice Krispies which "snap, crackle and pop," or Pop Rocks, the candy that created an outrageous fad because it literally popped in your mouth. M&Ms have become one of the most popular candies of all time with a positioning all children remember. "It melts in your mouth, not in your hands."

New soft gum was introduced to children as a more delicious bubble gum with brand names such as Bubble-Yum and Bubblicious. The product had a unique soft texture and was ideal for blowing bubbles.

EMPHASIZE FUN

No matter how you position the product, emphasize that special ingredient kids call *fun*. If a product isn't much fun, or doesn't have that special ingredient, then either direct it to a different market or junk it. There is no hope for it as a kids' product.

Over and over again, looking at hundreds of children's television commercials, it is easily apparent that children respond to the fun in any aspect of product advertising. It must be fun to do, fun to eat, fun to drink, fun to wear, or fun to look at. Frivolous and simplistic though it sounds, if you don't make it fun, it won't appeal to kids.

Sometimes seemingly ordinary things can be made more fun by the way you look at them, how you package them, or even the story you tell about them. For example, a candy product in Canada called "Smartees" took some rather ordinary but colorful candy-coated chocolate bits and made them much more fun on television. The candies came in various colors—reds, yellows, greens, blacks, browns, and whites. The product advertising was presented in an up-tempo jingle and showed the candies in a way kids loved, with a child doing something any child might do with candy but probably wouldn't occur to adults. The jingle merely asked, "When you eat your Smartees, do you eat the red ones last?"

One of the ways we made Burger Chef restaurants into a more fun place for kids was to transform the ordinary hamburger into a "Fun-burger" and a hamburger, drink, and french fries into a "Funmeal." It was all done with packaging. The "Funburger" came in a wrapper with a smiling face on it and was packed in a box printed with cartoons, games, and puzzles. The "Funmeal" was packed in a tray that had die-cut pop-outs and pop-ups. The trays changed every month or so and kids took items home to spend time with, just as they would a book of games and/or puzzles.

Recall the case of Rolos that Hershey's introduced. Chocolate-covered caramels that came in a protective tube was the product. On television, the tube became giant-sized and the Rolos came dancing out of the tube and performed a funny, fun-filled vaudeville act.

CHILDREN LIKE TO FEEL MORE GROWN-UP

Children like products that make them feel superior or more grown-up. The success of many products has been based on a positioning that allows children to pretend they are more grown-up.

Boys are concerned about power and strength. Hot Wheels are popular because they embody the wish to drive Dad's car, or perhaps even a more glamorous car than Dad is willing to try—certainly at speeds which only the most courageous driver would dare risk on a track.

One of Mattel's latest hit products for boys is a line of fantasy characters called He-Man and Masters of the Universe. The product not only has superhero figures, but ugly super-villains, too, and the product's accoutrements—vehicles, castles, dungeons, and traps—allow the child to act out the fantasy of the Superhero defeating the Bad Guys. All the superhero figures for boys such as Superman, Batman, Spiderman, and their latter day clone—the Six-Million Dollar Man are merely springboards to the fantasy of fighting the forces of evil by power and strength.

Girls are concerned with looks and cuteness. One of Barbie's most popular products was a kit of make-up and hairstyles girls could use on a large sculptured head-form of Barbie. Rather than make themselves up, girls preferred the fantasy of making Barbie more beautiful, something they might do for themselves when more grown-up.

Girls can also identify with Mom's role. Witness the recent success of the Cabbage Patch dolls, which appealed to every little girl's protective sense in wanting to adopt a poor little orphan.

The Adult Put-on

Some types of products can be positioned as an adult put-on. Children love to put on the adult world. They love to make fun of adults and see adults look stupid. Good-natured fun at the expense of the establishment puts the product in sympathy with the child's viewpoint. The product allows the child to pretend or fantasize he or she is on an equal footing with adults, even smarter.

Years ago, Mattel manufactured a candy-making machine for kids. A kind of sticky syrup was poured into molds and heated slightly with a lamp bulb. Out came a flexible, chewy candy in a number of forms. The forms themselves were really the appeal of the product. There were insects, worms, spiders, toads, beetles, and scorpions. The candy was unrealistically colorful; the shapes and forms were thoroughly revolting. But even more disgusting, they were edible. Mattel called the product "Incredible Edibles."

There was nothing very delicious about the candy. In fact, it didn't taste very good at all, probably why the product didn't last for more than a few years. But for two successive seasons the approach on television made this product one of the hits of the toy world. We merely showed children shocking adults by eating this candy in front of them.

The commercial was a quick series of vignettes of children eating worms in front of a man having his lunch, eating bug sandwiches, eating spiders with obvious relish, even offering an ice cream cone covered with caterpillars to a dog that runs away in fright. The adult reactions to the children's antics are what made the commercial so appealing to kids. It was also genuinely funny. The introductory commercial won an award for the funniest commercial produced in the world in that year.

Hershey's took a similar positioning when they introduced Reese's Peanut Butter Cups to children. The combination of peanut butter and chocolate was a unique taste. They brought them together on television in humorous slapstick situations in which an adult eating a chocolate bar somehow bumped into, fell on, slipped, or tripped on something causing a chocolate bar to collide with a jar of peanut butter being eaten by a child—all seemingly an accident. Each complains, "you got peanut butter on my chocolate" or "you got chocolate on my peanut butter." Then they both find the combination of tastes remarkably pleasant. The slapstick collisions and falls by clumsy adults made the commercials funny to kids.

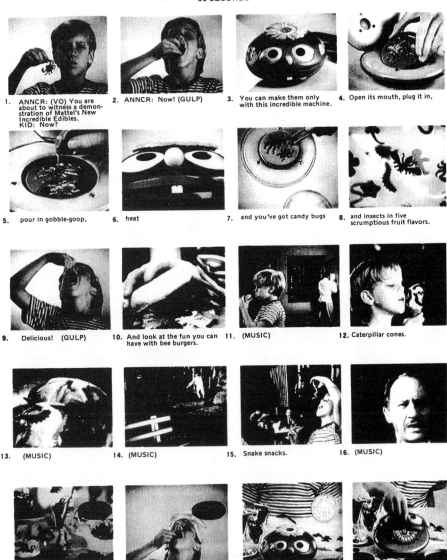

1. ANNCR: (VO) You are about to witness a demonstration of Mattel's New Incredible Edibles. KID: Now?
2. ANNCR: Now! (GULP)
3. You can make them only with this incredible machine.
4. Open its mouth, plug it in,
5. pour in gobble-goop,
6. heat
7. and you've got candy bugs
8. and insects in five scrumptious fruit flavors.
9. Delicious! (GULP)
10. And look at the fun you can have with bee burgers.
11. (MUSIC)
12. Caterpillar cones.
13. (MUSIC)
14. (MUSIC)
15. Snake snacks.
16. (MUSIC)
17. Mattel's New Incredible Edibles. Candy so pure, it has Good Housekeeping's seal.
18. (GULP)
19. Get Mattel's New Incredible Edibles. Incredible...
20. because they're edible. (MUSIC OUT)

Mattel's Incredible Edibles was positioned as an adult put-on. This commercial won an award for the funniest commercial produced in the world that year. The product was also a great, but short-lived, success. (Courtesy, Mattel Inc.)

DON'T LECTURE

While children want product information, the last thing they want on television is a lecture. They've heard enough in school that day. In their time with television they want to be entertained—which is not to say you cannot present an educational message. You can if you present it in an entertaining way or in a way to which kids can relate. The way Mattel's Talking Books were shown on television illustrates an identifiable situation for kids. A preschool youngster is shown playing with his talking books in a rather stuffy library. The voices from the books disturb other adult readers and a stern librarian stops the child's play. The child leaves the library with his books while the announcer says "Johnny hasn't learned to read yet, but he's beginning to like books. Mattel has made a library of talking books, so he can start his own library."

Many doll commercials show children pretending to be like Mom. The whole play situation of care, bathing, rocking, and diapering is an educational one, but children accept it as entertainment, an expression of how much fun can be obtained playing with the doll.

NAMING THE PRODUCT

Sometimes naming the product can become one of the most important factors in positioning it. If possible, the name should be closely compatible with the product. It should also connote fun, what the product is, or most importantly, what it does. How you present it can help tell children how to use it.

Here are some names of children's products that function exceedingly well: Baby Thataway, Chatty Cathy, Baby Alive, Pebbles, Spaghetti-O's, Cheerios, Alpha-Bits, Bubble-Yum, Bubblicious, Care Bears, Fruit Loops, Crispy Critters.

TALKING TO PARENTS ABOUT KIDS' PRODUCTS

When you position a child's product to an adult, you must tell them what it will do for the child. Some types of children's products are more interesting to adults than to the preschool children who use them. Tell a mother (and grandmothers and relatives) what benefit her child will

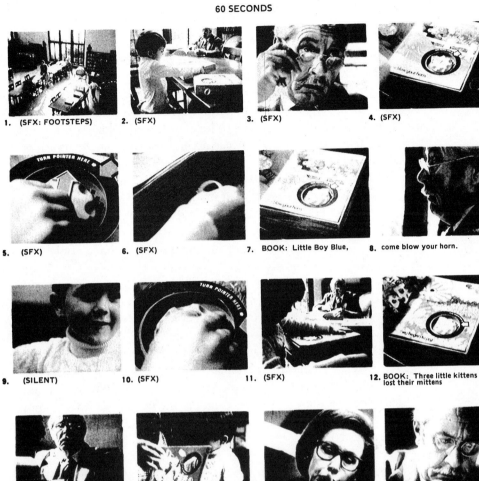

1. (SFX: FOOTSTEPS)

2. (SFX)

3. (SFX)

4. (SFX)

5. (SFX)

6. (SFX)

7. BOOK: Little Boy Blue,

8. come blow your horn.

9. (SILENT)

10. (SFX)

11. (SFX)

12. BOOK: Three little kittens
lost their mittens

13. and they began

14. to cry.

15. WOMAN: Shhh!

16. (SILENT)

17. ANNCR: (VO) Johnny
hasn't learned to read, yet,
but he's beginning to like
books.

18. To encourage him, Mattel has
made a library of talking
story books

19. so he can start his own
library.

20. (SFX)

Some types of children's products are more interesting to adults than to the children who use them. A good example is Mattel's Talking Book, which makes an amusing point about a child learning to read. (Courtesy, Mattel Inc.)

receive from the product and assure her about such attributes as safety, durability, and nutrition. In researching preschool toy products, parents will always tell you the most important attribute in a toy is that it be safe. They also want a preschool product to be durable—able to stand up to inordinate punishment. These are legitimate and rational concerns. That a child can learn from some products is also valuable. What mothers will seldom articulate is any concern about the play value or appeal of the toy to the child. In these areas, her judgment becomes less certain. What parents find difficult to express in research is their dilemma about which product to buy because of their uncertainty regarding the child's interests. Preschool children are not as articulate about what they want or have seen on television. They ask for so many things, it is difficult to discriminate between what they really want and those toys which have only momentary appeal.

The one thing every parent, grandparent, or relative wants to do is please the child. A gift of a toy is their expression of love for the child and they want the child's love and affection in return. If you've ever given a child a toy, ask yourself—would you miss the expression on the child's face when he opens the gift? Not on your life. It's an important moment for both of you because it's an emotion-filled situation. A rejection of the toy, which sometimes happens since younger children are not necessarily socialized to the point of receiving a gift politely, is an unhappy experience. So is a reaction of boredom. One feels the effort to express love has been wasted.

To be effective, advertising should be sensitive to this situation. To appeal to the adult's rational side, you must inform them about the values of the product that will be good for the child, but if you can also convince the viewer or reader that the child will be overjoyed with the product, it alleviates a great deal of unspoken concern.

There have been some classic examples of how these considerations have been combined into a single 30-second commercial. Key product points were made, and the framework or situation of the commercial touched the emotional considerations.

We made a commercial for Mattel about a talking clock, an educational product for preschoolers. The toy was helpful in learning to tell time—apparently not much fun for kids, but very appealing to adults. The commercial showed a father telling his youngster what the big hand signified, and then what the little hand signified. The father was attempting to teach the child to read the face of a clock and doing it badly. The child was confused, the father frustrated. He turns to the camera and asks for "help!" The solution, naturally, was the Talking Clock, and subsequent

1. FATHER: Got it?

2. BOY: Yeah, it's 15 o'clock.

3. FATHER: Uh, no son. When the 3 is 15, it's a quarter of an hour;

4. when the 3 is an hour, then the 3 is a 3. See?

5. ANNCR: (VO) Sometimes

6. parents can use a little help,

7. like the new Mattel-A-Time Talking Clock.

8. CLOCK: The time is 3 o'clock.

9. ANNCR: (VO) It tells the time

10. for every 5 minutes of the day.

11. BOY AND CLOCK: The time is 7:05.

12. ANNCR: (VO) The new Talking Clock from Mattel.

The commercial for Mattel's Talking Clock is directed at adults. It takes a familiar situation of teaching a child to tell time and shows how the toy can by helpful. (Courtesy, Mattel Inc.)

101

scenes showed a child having fun learning and a father beaming with pride. The points of the product were displayed and an emotionally satisfied adult was depicted in an entirely familiar, believable situation.

Hershey's used the same concept with Reese's Peanut Butter Cups. A mother is shown getting ready for the kids to rush in after school. She is preparing their snack. She points out that the product is highly nutritious, and while she prattles on about the vitamin content, the kids rush in noisily and expectantly and go off obviously enjoying the product. Simple, but effective.

Kool-Aid uses similar situations. While Mom talks about Vitamin C, all the kids in the neighborhood come over. She is the favorite Mom on the block.

This two-pronged approach to adults, explaining that the product is good as well as fun for kids, is the strategy we used in marketing Nickelodeon, the first cable channel for kids. When the network was first started, we were pioneering for cable subscribers, and this advertising approach convinced parents to hook up Nickelodeon in their homes via cable television. Here was a product that grew, in just a few years, to achieve more than 26 million subscribers, because adults perceived the need for better quality television for their kids—not necessarily because children demanded it.

Sales Promotions for Kids

Sales promotions are aimed at achieving a sudden sales burst. Over the long haul they cannot sustain a brand, but if done correctly can provide an immediate lift. Generally, sales promotions must offer something for free, at a reduced price, or something extra beyond the product. When doing sales promotions for kids, you must offer something kids really want. Something free or at a reduced price simply isn't enough. Kids must genuinely want what you're offering because you are asking them to act immediately.

Research with kids is the only way you can plan a sales promotion with any degree of certainty. Certain factors must be considered. On-pack premiums, for example, are far better than mail-ins. Kids want instant gratification and won't usually make the extra effort required to fill out a coupon and mail it. If they do make an effort, by the time the premium arrives in the mail, they are no longer interested.

An example of a successful sales promotion for children is one we did for Burger Chef. We offered a hamburger, drink, and french fries on a special plate—a flying saucer that could be used as a Frisbee. Buy the food, keep the plate. The television commercial showed children stepping out of Burger Chef's and hurling their plates in the parking lot. Sales jumped as much as 20 percent in the markets using the promotion.

A big or important offer has the potential of exploding beyond all expectations. If happens only rarely, but an advertiser must be prepared to fulfill the offer quickly even if it exceeds the estimated response. Once in a Mattel promotion, we offered boys a special silver car, the "Boss Hoss Special," for only $1.00. This particular Hot Wheels model was not available in stores and could only be obtained through the promotional offer. (Incidentally, this is an interesting technique in making a product more desirable.) We expected to fulfill 150,000 orders; instead we had orders for 1.5 million. Caught short on supply, new die-cast tooling had to be made to manufacture that many cars and more than a million children were kept waiting months for their special car. Parents phoned and wrote, feeling their child was ripped off. Suffice to say, the success of the promotion created a troublesome mess. One way to avoid this problem is to limit the number of special offers and announce that number in the offer. Point out that only so many are available and will be provided to the first-comers. The most successful promotion in Mattel history was handled that way. The Barbie Trade-in limited its introductory offer to 1,250,000 dolls.

Some Techniques of Execution

As well as fun, try to make television commercials for children funny. For children, broad ridiculous humor is funnier than puns or wordplay. Visual, physical humor always works best. A slip on a banana peel always works, especially if an adult is the butt of the joke. So do gross food jokes if they can be used appropriately within a commercial (for example, Incredible Edibles). The entire repertoire of slapstick jokes from vaudeville and the silent movies is a rich mine of visual humor kids still love.

These gags also work well in animation. They are easier to do in this technique and kids are used to seeing this type of outrageous visual humor in such favorite cartoon classics as "Tom and Jerry," "Bugs Bunny," and "Roadrunner." Violence must be toned down, but speed, imaginative pratfalls, collisions, and funny sound effects can still achieve harmless humor. Years ago we did a classic version of this technique for Baskin-Robbins 31 Flavors ice cream. It was completely animated and combined slapstick with the standard pie (ice cream) in the face and ridiculous flavors (rhinoceros ice cream). Kids never tired of seeing this particular commercial and found something new to laugh about each time it was played.

MONSTER SPOOFS

Jokes about monsters seem to be sure-fire when done correctly. One can always find ways to make such monsters as Frankenstein, Dracula, King Kong, and Godzilla into silly, non-threatening characters. Just the fact that they are seen out of character is funny to kids. General Mills bases Count Chocula and Frankenberry cereals wholly on this premise. The all-time, highest test score commercial for General Foods was for Burger Chef, introducing a wild character called Fangburger, a Count Dracula look-alike who liked to drop into Burger Chef just for a "bite." The kids thought the funniest of these was when Fangburger brought in his wife and kids, all Dracula look-alikes.

STAY IN THE CHILD'S CULTURAL WORLD

A common mistake in children's commercials is to rely on the adult frame of reference. Research with children spotlights these mistakes over and over again. For example, today's kids have never heard of or seen Harold Lloyd, Tom Mix, or Charlie Chaplin. These visual icons do not call up the same treasure trove of memories as they do for adults. Only a few of yesteryear's favorites are still recognized by most children. For example, kids still know Frankenstein's monster, Dracula, King Kong, and Godzilla, but no other monster in our popular culture means anything to them. Maybe a handful of children have seen reissues of the Our Gang comedies and the Shirley Temple films, but they are far from popular with today's generation of youngsters.

If humor is to be achieved by satire, it must make reference to a common experience or character type familiar to all. But if you are going to use satire with children, it must be done obviously, broadly, and be about subject matter with which they are intimate. Unless it's done extremely well, it's a good idea to thoroughly test this technique with a children's audience. And if you are looking to be safe, it's a good idea to avoid this technique altogether. There are other ways to make kids laugh.

The Use of Children's Language

It is obvious that children do not use the same jargon as adults. Their language reflects a child's changing view of the world. Even if you have listened closely and believe you understand the nuances of a child's language, when talking to a child on television resist the temptation to talk in his slang. First of all, you will probably do it badly. Secondly, they don't believe adults talk that way and they resent the intrusion into their world.

If you use slang in talk between one child and another, you must be very careful. Much of children's slang is regional, some confined just to particular neighborhoods or schools. What you hear your own kids say continuously might not register in another part of the same city, not to speak of another region of the country.

Test Alternative Sound Tracks

The testing of alternative sound tracks on commercials will reveal some interesting phenomena. Many things you might believe would never show up, will surface with surprising regularity. You will discover that most boys prefer to hear men tell them things. Girls respond to male announcers only if they sound warm and friendly and remind them of their fathers. If the commercial is for a girl's product and the nature of the product is essentially female (a girl's doll) then a woman's voice will do fine.

What is particularly tricky is the use of children's voices, on or off camera. Children's voices, particularly on camera, are wonderfully humorous and warm to adults. Countless successful commercials using children as spokespersons have charmed adults on television. The use of children's voices on or off camera adds warmth and authenticity to children's commercials as well, but in this case their use is riskier. Children's voices are often thin, tinny, and squeaky. Copy points get lost because they are garbled or inaudible and you find yourself going back into your commercials to rerecord and dub in clearer voices, which may sound very artificial. Only if you are sure you can get what you need from a child actor/actress and have time in the production schedule to try it repeatedly, is it worth the risk. Remember, most of the time the child actor/actress can only work a half-day.

There are also dangers in using foreign or ethnic humor. Don't assume children will understand a foreign accent unless you have checked it out, and the sensitive advertiser today should avoid ethnic stereotypes.

Black, Hispanic, Jewish, or Italian accents are generally in poor taste. Television programming uses ethnic characters constantly, and consequently the temptations for humor and authenticity are part of the medium. They can make a point quickly when anything else seems to avoid reality. A foreign flavor need not add up to an ethnic slur.

For example, we once did a new game commercial for Mattel that involved a team of German scientists competing against a team of chimpanzees. The scientists were played very broadly and looked like the standard German scientists kids were accustomed to seeing in movies. The explanation of the action was given by an off-camera announcer, and he, too, had a German accent. Testing revealed that kids did not understand the announcer or the attempts at humor made in the sound track. When we changed the announcer to a standard American voice, the commercial scored highly with children.

KIDS RELATE TO OTHER KIDS ON TELEVISION

Kids relate to other kids they see on television. They either like or reject them. The situations they see them in either ring true or don't. Beware of artificial play situations. They are deadly and kids spot them immediately. Test scores for a commercial involving a Little League baseball team were extremely low. The commercial showed a Little League team getting off a bus after a ball game. Because their uniforms were still clean, the kids in the audience didn't believe the kids had played ball at all. Consequently nothing else in the commercial was believed.

The wrong kids create disbelief as well. Children relate to children who are like themselves. They recognize children who might be their friends, neighbors, or classmates.

Some years ago a West Coast headquartered fast-food chain, named Jack-in-the Box, used a child spokesman named Rodney Allen Rippy. He was a particularly cute youngster who charmed both adults and kids because he made obvious mistakes on camera. He simply didn't appear to be a professional performer, but just another kid. He became a popular celebrity in the regions where his commercials ran. He was a kid's favorite wherever he appeared.

At the same time, a pool of commercials appeared on national television for Underwood's Deviled Ham. They too used a child spokesman— but of a different sort. The child's name was Mason Reese and he was an exceptionally precocious television salesman. He, too, was charming and funny, but only for adults. Tests revealed that kids hated Mason Reese.

Testing also reveals how sensitive you must be in play situations. Don't show an eight-year-old boy playing with an eight-year-old girl. For boys, that's an unreal situation. Girls will emulate boys, but boys will not emulate girls. When in doubt, use boys.

Don't show an older activity in the hands of a younger child. Older children will turn-off instantly, unlike younger children who identify with older ones. When in doubt, cast older.

Make sure your kid characters are groomed and attired correctly. The children's identification system is constantly changing. In both dress and hairstyles, avoid any extreme.

A few years back a commercial was tested in which a boy wore high-topped sneakers. Because he wasn't wearing the low, colorful athletic type, the boy was immediately labelled a nerd by child viewers. If the same commercial were tested today, the boy would be considered very with-it because high-tops are back in fashion.

THE IMPORTANCE OF SOUND

Sound is particularly important to children. Rhythm and rhyme can help product message retention. Children like and remember catchy tunes and tricky combinations of words. They can repeat slogans and jingles and unusual phrases—sometimes not knowing what they mean.

It isn't coincidence that the creators of popular children's characters have continually used a saying or a phrase identified solely with their characters. It helps children remember what they see. Joe Barbera coined "Yabba Dabba Doo" for Fred Flintstone, and "Smarter than the average bear" for Yogi Bear. Everyone still remembers the Lone Ranger's "Hiyo Silver," and Orphan Annie's exclamation to her dog, "Gloriosky." Even Tarzan's familiar jungle call is remembered. My former partner, Jack Roberts, understood the importance of this concept when he coined "You can tell it's Mattel, it's swell." You heard it every time you saw the Mattel logo. It wasn't used to convince anyone that Mattel was swell. It was used so kids would remember Mattel's trademark. Years after it was introduced, kids who couldn't even read the words in the trademark, could identify Mattel's red serrated seal by sight. They said, "That's a Mattel."

Music in commercials does not always have to be what the kids are currently listening to. Any music with a beat and a simple structure will work without sounding out-of-date or old-fashioned. Country songs are easy to remember. One of the most effective jingle soundtracks I ever heard was a song based on a fugue. As the music built up, so did the contagion of the commercial.

The temptation is always to show the latest in styles, music, and dancing. Inexperienced young creative people are scared that children will feel their communication with them is square. They often forget that rapping and break dancing might go over well in Los Angeles and New York, but in Iowa the freckle-faced kids are still down at the soda fountain getting a sundae or out playing Little League baseball. And these activities will remain long after video rock and all its popularity has been forgotten.

The "Money Shot"

Every commercial for children should have at least one motivating scene. Some cynics in the trade have referred to this as the *money shot*. Here are a few suggestions for the motivating scene:

1. A premium that comes with the product. It can come in the box like it does with some cereals or can be an offer of free prizes for writing in.

2. News is especially important. News can illustrate features for a new product or focus on an old product in which something new has been added. Kids perk up to news that interests them.

3. Product demonstration. Children are especially fond of appetizing close-ups of food: a pie being cut in half, syrup pouring over ice cream, creamy peanut butter being spread, or a frosty glass of soda.

4. Show someone children admire enjoying the product.

5. Someone else wanting the product is motivating. But you must be careful here. The wanting person must not be underprivileged and the holder of the product more privileged. This makes a social statement that might be injurious to less fortunate children. A fantasy or cartoon works best for this technique. For example, the standard story line for General Food's Pebbles cereal is Fred Flintstone trying to get the cereal away from his friend Barney, or vice versa. The situations are often humorous and motivating, and they make the cereal more fun.

Testing Commercials

The suggestions I've made for communicating with children are not to be taken as if they were absolute, concrete, sure-fire rules to follow. Experience with creating and testing more than 1,000 commercials for kids tells one a great deal, but there are always surprises. Certain areas are often unclear even though they've been tested several times. The reason for this is the unreliability of test data from children. Feedback from tests with children is always a little hazy.

Testing commercials with children is difficult to say the least. Because younger children can't read or write, they can only give answers based on a scale of smiling to frowning faces. And, of course, verbal communication is severely limited. Older children do not communicate their thoughts clearly and are at a stage when they are strongly influenced by the setting in which they are tested. The test situation is always very unnatural. For example, in a group of six children who do not know one another, a leader emerges more quickly than it would if they were adults. The other children will look to the one they admire before answering. Desire for approval often dictates their opinions. Testing with parents in the room is out of the question. Parents are so eager for their child to make a good showing that they tend to interrupt and kibitz, influencing the children in the room.

It is possible to achieve reliable results using a variety of techniques, but adult techniques, such as recall, are not reliable. It is amazing that many large sophisticated advertisers are still trying to get some meaningful information using day after recall methods with children. Children can barely feed back what they have just seen.

The biggest problem in testing commercials with children is separating the product from the commercial. Children, especially young children, have difficulty separating their reactions to a specific commercial from their evaluation of the product advertised. The commercial, for them, is the product. Therefore, when advertising to children, the commercial and the product must be totally consistent. The product must live up to the commercial, and the commercial must faithfully represent the product.

If the commercial and product are appealing and receive wide acceptance, the best advertising will be word of mouth. Verbal contagion can make a children's product successful. Conversely, disappointed children can kill a product with astonishing speed. When disappointed with a product, children quickly tell parents and friends. These products are rapidly assigned to the "I'll never buy that again" trash bin. The best products and the best commercials are those that live up to their advertising promises.

Advertising to children should, above all, be honest. It should present product messages in clear and relevant ways children can understand and relate to. To do that, you must understand children and their needs. Studying children with continuing research, questioning, and probing is the only means of creating good communication with children. Through a variety of special research techniques you can learn by watching and listening to children. While no testing is sure-fire or absolute, you must find out as much as you can by testing your message as it is seen through the eyes of children. And because of the difficulty in extracting very exact data, the information must be continually shared in a free-flowing dialogue between the researchers and the creative people whose work is being judged and who must correct and revise it if it goes astray.

CHAPTER 5

The Licensed Character— Today's Hottest Salesman

TOYS BECOME TELEVISION SHOWS

OVER THE PAST COUPLE OF YEARS, THE LONGSTANDING CONNECTION BETWEEN television and licensed merchandise has taken a purportedly new twist. New children's characters are no longer originated by television or movies. Instead they are originated by toy companies as products, then turned into television shows. Some recent examples follow:

- "He-Man and Masters of the Universe," 65 half-hours in national syndication based on a line of products made by Mattel.

- "G.I. Joe," first a mini-series in national syndication. Now a 65 half-hour series based on a long-standing line of products from Hasbro.

- "The Gobots," a 65 half-hour series in syndication based on a line of toys from Tonka.

- "Transformers," a 65 half-hour series in syndication based on a successful toy line from Hasbro.

- "She-Ra: Princess of Power," a spinoff of "He-Man and Masters of the Universe." She-Ra is He-Man's sister and is featured in a 65 half-hour series based on a line of products from Mattel.

"He-Man and the Masters of the Universe" is a 65 half-hour animated show based on a line of products from Mattel. This show and product line became one of the all-time licensing hits of the toy industry. (Copyright: 1983 Filmation Associates, Inc. Characters © Mattel, Inc.; all rights reserved. He-Man and Masters of the Universe are trademarks of Mattel, Inc. Used with permission.)

The theory behind these new shows is that young viewers have already been attracted to the characters in toy form, and will therefore be attracted to the programs. Conversely, the programs help boost retail sales of the existing and new products in these brand categories. A switch in the traditional order of progression has occurred. The product or concept has entered the framework of children's culture before becoming a movie or television program. In essence, programs become half-hour commercials for an existing brand.

This bevy of new shows has attracted attention from critics who complain that these programs are nothing more than long-form commercials. Two consumerist groups, Action for Children's Television (ACT) and the National Coalition of Television Violence, have made the loudest complaints. ACT has filed a complaint with the FCC, but so far nothing significant has arisen from the complaints. Given the current climate at the FCC, it will probably all blow over after a suitable period of apathy.

THE HALF-HOUR COMMERCIAL ISN'T NEW

The idea of creating television shows from existing properties or stories is not new. Many television shows and movies are preceded by a book, play, or an existing mythical character. Making a children's television show from toys isn't even new. It's almost as old as conventional commercials although its form has been less common and less developed.

In 1969, Eddie Smardan, my associate at Carson/Roberts, developed a "Hot Wheels" program based on Mattel's Hot Wheels line of miniature cars. Prior to that, General Foods had created shows starring Sugar Bear and Linus the Lionhearted, both character spokesmen for their cereals.

The FCC challenged the "Hot Wheels" series aired on ABC on Saturday morning. ABC rejected the notion that the show or the transaction was wrong. They stated they had no prior sponsor commitment for the show from Mattel, that Mattel was not running their Hot Wheels commercials within the show, and that the show was merely designed on a hot new concept popular with kids. The National Association of Broadcasters (NAB), a lobbying group for the broadcast industry, also backed the network and indicated this program should not concern the FCC. In 1970, the FCC indicated their disapproval to ABC, but did not cancel the show.

Frankly, the whole argument is a little bit like the chicken and the egg. Obviously, no one complains when television shows or movies breed new licensing ideas for products. This has been going on for 40 years. But when the product comes *before* television shows, then it's viewed as a commercial.

In my mind, except for possible weaknesses in story lines and character development in these shows, the results are not much different. Product ideas are often built into shows anyway. If entertainment creators anticipate a television show or movie is going to succeed with children, the show's creators almost always design elements in the entertainment that they can later license for manufacturing. This element is as much a part of the revenue for an entertainment product as are the fees charged to exhibitors or networks for the rights to play the show. All these factors are considered during production, if not earlier.

I learned this lesson in 1955 when Mattel first sponsored "The Mickey Mouse Club." Because "The Mickey Mouse Club" was a hot show, it was natural to make Mickey Mouse Club merchandise for kids. Mattel made a musical guitar called the "Mousegetar." They developed a "Mouse Kartooner" that helped kids draw cartoons. And they made a Mickey Mouse Club Newsreel that played 10-framed film strips from Disney films along with an accompanying record. (I personally wrote and produced the filmstrips and the records directly from the Disney programs.)

Mattel's owners quickly realized that the Disney Company was getting very rich on the five percent royalty it received for every product sold carrying the Disney name. Elliot Handler resented every nickel of royalty and decided to develop his own characters on television or get the rights to them. Over the next 25 years, Mattel did exactly that.

After "The Mickey Mouse Club," the agency developed Matty Mattel and Sister Belle, two characters who hosted a cartoon show called "Matty's Funday Funnies." Carson/Roberts negotiated the merchandising rights to "Beany & Cecil" for Mattel before the advertiser would fully sponsor the show on the ABC network for two years. The same situation occurred with NBC and "Flipper." And Barbie, of course, Mattel licensed to more than 100 other manufacturers who paid Mattel five percent of their wholesale sales price for the right to use the name on their products. Many of those Barbie licenses started in the early '60s and continue today. Mattel's "He-Man and the Masters of the Universe" represents the number one example of this supposedly new phenomenon.

The Explosive Growth of Licensing

Looking back on it, all those early licensing activities in the '50s and '60s were, forgive the expression, child's play compared to activities today. According to a survey from 1983 by *The Licensing Letter,* a trade newsletter to the licensing industry, licensed merchandise generated $26.7 billion in retail sales during 1982. In 1986 estimates indicated that licensing had grown to more than $40 billion in retail sales.

During the '50s and '60s the licensing industry was barely in its infancy, nowhere near the bonanza it is today. There is a greater proliferation of licensed merchandise today than at any other time in history. Manufacturers of toys, apparel, sporting goods, food, greeting cards, paper goods, and every sort of novelty item have become acutely aware of the appeal of goods themed to the latest hit movie or television show.

It Started With Star Wars

In 1977 the licensing industry took a giant leap forward and has been growing by enormous jumps ever since. One factor, more than any other, suddenly changed things—the success of the motion picture *Star Wars.*

This film, one of the greatest blockbusters in movie history, along with George Lucas's subsequent films in the *Star Wars* series (*The Empire Strikes Back* and *Return of the Jedi*), and his more recent pictures (*Raiders of the Lost Ark* and *Indiana Jones and the Temple of Doom*) have generated more than $2 billion in licensed product sales. Never in character merchandising history has there been anything quite like it. This success changed the face and nature of the licensing business for years to come.

In 1976 licensed toys accounted for 20 percent of all toy sales. By 1977 it had climbed to 33 percent. Today almost 80 percent of toy sales are of licensed products. For the past seven or eight years, licensed products became the year's hits, for example, *Star Wars* figures, Six Million Dollar Man, Strawberry Shortcake, Care Bears, He-Man, and the like. The phenomenon is so important in marketing today, so crucial to the success of a children's product, one would think this sales technique was just invented, that the industry had, like discovering gold, suddenly discovered a new way to thrill the youngsters of today. That's hardly the case. Licensing has been practiced, albeit at a quiet level, for more than 70 years. The first licensed product for children was introduced in 1913 when the Ideal Toy Company secured permission from President Teddy Roosevelt to manufacture and sell the Teddy Bear. President Roosevelt used the royalties to set up a network of national parks. Five years later the licensing of Raggedy Ann surfaced, and in 1928 Walt Disney introduced Mickey Mouse to America.

Since that time, thousands of other personalities and characters have been used as licensed or franchised properties, and as such have become salesmen for hundreds of billions of dollars worth of merchandise.

Mickey Mouse, the greatest salesman of them all, is approaching his 60th birthday. Buck Rogers is well over 50 years old; so are the Lone Ranger and Dick Tracy. Conversely, thousands of other characters and promoted properties have had only momentary fame and consequently a more limited appeal in the marketplace.

THE FIVE CRUCIAL INGREDIENTS FOR SUCCESS

From my own experience and analysis of this phenomenon over its first 65 years, I learned that it takes a combination of five special ingredients to make a million-dollar licensed character. I have also learned in the last few years, while these five special ingredients remain vital, the momentum and overflowing popularity of character merchandise has created exceptions to

Mickey Mouse, the greatest salesman of them all, is approaching his 60th birthday. He has always been seen as the all-American nice guy. (Copyright © The Walt Disney Company)

the five principles and a few of these exceptions are beginning to create some sketchy new principles of their own. I will discuss these new developments later, but first let's examine what has traditionally been tried and true.

1. *The property or character must appeal to children.* Children are the key market, and children are far and away the largest group of consumers of this merchandise. The middle-aged childs (five-twelve) is the most important group, followed by the 13-18, then the two-five range, and lastly, infants to age two. Consequently, the most successful properties or characters are geared to the relative intelligence, educational level, media exposure, and cultural influences of this first target age group. Few valuable properties are very complicated or sophisticated.

2. *There must be media exposure.* Thirty to 40 years ago newspaper comic strips, comic books, radio, and movies had sufficient media weight to make a character popular. Today, even a tremendous hit movie might not do the job unless the movie has an enormous media budget for television advertising.

3. *The character or property must have the right ingredients.* The ones that come directly from the mainstream of popular American culture seem to create recognition, familiarity, and fame the fastest, and endure the longest.

4. *The character must be sold by an aggressive and knowledgeable licensing agent acutely aware of the need for the first three ingredients.* The licensing agent or company must know which customers to sell to and how to control the integrity and exclusivity of the license.

The best licensing agents are also marketers, and when key ingredients are missing from the mix, they know how to add them to insure success of licensed merchandise.

5. *The timing must be right.* Latching on to a hot licensed character is a little like catching a wave. Too early, no ride. Too late, a disaster. Just at the top of the crest, grabbing the momentum at the right moment, makes for an exciting and heady ride that can last for a couple of seasons.

Given the faddish and fickle nature of the children's market, deciding *what* is right *when* is more often intuitive than rational. The number of mistakes are legion.

As you might suspect, consumer recognition of a famous character or property does not happen fleetingly or by chance. Children are bombarded by so much in the media and exposed to so many personalities that superstar status can only be achieved by brilliant and original innovation, meticulous marketing, planning, and the most massive exposure.

THE STAR WARS STORY

Take *Star Wars,* for example. The film opened in May 1977 in 32 theaters. Every element of the film that eventually found its way to the marketplace was planned carefully in the film. When the film was first written and being prepared for production, it became apparent that the movie's colorful characters, robots, and gadgets would have incredible merchandising potential. Just after the film's release, 17 manufacturers signed up to make *Star Wars* merchandise. Kenner Toys was one of those licensees. They signed an exclusive world-wide toy and games agreement with 20th Century Fox and have since marketed a broad line of products including those for the *Star Wars* sequels, *The Empire Strikes Back* and *Return of the Jedi.* Their sales volume on these products was well into the hundreds of millions of dollars.

Twentieth Century Fox Studios, which released *Star Wars,* initially produced 650,000 albums of the sound track and sold millions. T-shirts and posters, merchandise that does not require tooling or extensive production expense, were released immediately and sold briskly. Almost immediately, *Star Wars* posters outsold Farrah Fawcett posters, then the hottest piece of paper goods on the market.

For Halloween, in *Star Wars'* first season, life-like masks of the movie characters including Luke Skywalker, Chewbacca, Darth Vader, the Imperial Storm Troopers, and the robot C3PO were sold in the thousands at $39.95 retail.

In retrospect, the substantial advance money Kenner had to pay 20th Century Fox for the right to make *Star Wars* merchandise doesn't seem like much of a gamble. There were a number of indications that the toys would become hot merchandise. At the time the deal was made, however, no one had any idea these movies would be such a whopping success, and some felt there was considerable risk in the venture. In fact, the same deal which Kenner made had been turned down by at least one other major toy company.

One must remember that at the time *Star Wars* was made, licensed products coming from hit movies had not been big winners. Historically speaking, that the merchandise from this movie took off the way it did represented an incredible bull's-eye on the part of Bernie Loomis, who was then president of Kenner Toys.

LICENSING FROM MOVIES IS LIMITED

In 1977, movies had not been the source of licensed merchandise that sold in enormous quantities. Other hits of that period, such as *Jaws* and *King Kong,* sold record albums, T-shirts, posters, buttons, and premium glasses and maybe an inexpensive game or two, but the real licensing gold mines sell toys, apparel, books, and food and continue to sell for years.

Mary Poppins was one of Walt Disney's hottest licensed properties. Forty-six different manufacturers licensed and produced Mary Poppins merchandise. (Copyright © 1964 The Walt Disney Company)

The first feature motion picture to license products for merchandising was Disney's *Snow White and the Seven Dwarfs* in 1937. By that time, Disney had eight or nine years of experience marketing its cartoon characters from shorts and the same companies licensing Mickey Mouse, Donald Duck, and the Three Little Pigs introduced products from *Snow White*. For the most part, they were products for girls like jewelry, clothing, card games, figurines, books, and sweatshirts.

After that, each Disney movie generated a new line of products, including *Pinocchio* and *Fantasia* in 1940, *Dumbo* in 1941, and *Bambi* in 1942, but none were as successful as *Snow White*. The next major licensing success from movies didn't happen until 1964 when Disney released *Mary Poppins*.

The film, based on the classic children's books by the Australian author Pamela Travers, was Walt Disney's biggest hit. It not only grossed $45 million on its first release, it provided Disney's Character Merchandis-

119

ing Division with the revenues from 46 manufacturers who were licensed to produce Mary Poppins merchandise. In addition to the usual inexpensive novelties, there were Mary Poppins dresses, underwear, sleepwear, gloves, mittens, robes, coats, coat and hat sets, dolls, stuffed toys, umbrellas, luggage, toy chests, dinner-wear, even shoe polish.

Obviously this movie had all the right ingredients for its time. Was there a five- to twelve-year-old little girl who didn't see it? I venture many of them saw it over and over again, creating not only the needed media exposure in terms of reach, but frequency as well.

Movies of that period and before seldom attracted so many different types of licensees. Even films many marketers thought would capture kids' imaginations, such as *Chitty-Chitty Bang-Bang, Doctor Doolittle,* and *Willie Wonka* (all based on perennially best-selling children's books) did not prove to be sales bonanzas for licensors. One exception during this time was *Planet of the Apes,* but that was a series of movies and a television show. The movie alone did not popularize the concept.

TELEVISION IS THE MOST INFLUENTIAL FORCE

Until *Star Wars* appeared in 1977 (followed by its sequels) television was the most influential force for creating licensed properties. In recent years television has been, and continues to be, a more predictable creator of merchandisable characters and ideas that sell goods in astronomical numbers over a long period. There has never been a force more powerful with children than the half-hour commercial when it plays regularly over several years. Television can do what movies cannot by virtue of its enormous reach and frequency of exposure, two vitally important elements in making a character for kids highly popular. These ideas communicated in television function in every way like product commercials. The same dynamics of family interchange and the predictable reactions to commercials by age and sex all function in the same way. In fact, many of the appeals and communication techniques we've learned how to use in television commercials have come from successful children's movies and vice versa.

The success of products and commercials can be either hit or miss on television, and the medium can be puzzling and deceptive for the maker of children's goods who is looking for a fresh idea for new products. At one time, some people believed a hit Saturday morning network show featuring a new character stood a good chance of being extraordinarily effective in helping to sell children's products. A closer look indicates that these shows have seldom been successful in creating new and original licensed characters, but can bolster and support an existing character once it has been established. Good examples are "Smurfs," "Mr. T.," and "Rubik's Cube" which all existed in either product form or in another medium before they went on Saturday morning.

Licensors are finding that a new character can be more easily created by syndicated specials or a syndicated series than by Saturday morning network television. There's good reason for this fact. In peak season and at peak times, the homes watching Saturday morning network programming number approximately 18 million. (Surprisingly, nearly 30 percent of these homes have no children under 12.) This total audience is split three ways so that even a hit show reaches only six million homes per week, and only one time. Even if the show is a half-hour commercial, this amount of exposure is simply inadequate—in terms of reach and frequency—to make an individual character tremendously popular.

Expectation of success from Saturday morning network television alone is tantamount to expecting success from a campaign consisting of one or two national commercials per week on a Saturday show. We have learned that television responsive products require an 80 to 90 percent reach (almost all the children in the target age group) with an average frequency of at least five times. (Heavy viewers would see the commercial about ten times in this type of schedule.)

The reach and frequency of a Saturday morning show is sometimes expanded considerably after the show has played its run on network for a year or two (sometimes considerably longer) and then placed into syndication. If enough episodes of the show have been made, it is often programmed by local stations as a week-day strip and many children see the half-hour show five times per week, rather than once. If there is a line-up of stations covering 75 percent or more of the country, then cumulative homes per week can run as high as 16.5 million for one show, particularly if the ratings for the show hold up well.

Years ago it was possible for a Saturday morning show to end up on a network in an entirely different time slot, such as 7:00 or 7:30 P.M. (EST). That built a much larger audience. One particular arrangement was made in the late '50s with ABC for Mattel to sponsor two shows: "Matty's Funday Funnies" and "Funday Funnies with Beany and Cecil." ABC played the shows twice a week, on Saturday morning and then on Sunday evenings. The hefty nighttime audience accounted for the popularity of Casper the Friendly Ghost and the Beany and Cecil merchandise that came as a direct result of those shows.

PRIME TIME IS BEST

Prime-time shows reach even larger numbers of homes and children under 12 than Saturday morning shows do. Here are some typical statistics on prime-time kid shows over the years (in millions).

PROGRAM	NUMBER OF HOMES	NUMBER OF CHILDREN (AGED 2 TO 11)
"Happy Days"	23.4 homes	15.7 children
"Six Million Dollar Man"	20.8 homes	14.1 children
"Bionic Woman"	16.5 homes	10.8 children
"Donny & Marie"	15.5 homes	10.1 children
"Mork & Mindy"	19.6 homes	10.5 children
"Battlestar Galactica"	17.7 homes	9.6 children
"A-Team"	21.0 homes	14.6 children
"Dukes of Hazzard"	19.0 homes	9.9 children

Coincidentally, all of the above shows were, or still are, hot licensing properties, and merchandise inspired by the personalities in these shows did well in the marketplace. Any one of them might have done even better had they contained all of the ingredients necessary for a big licensing hit, but they had enough good characters and enough exposure to qualify as best sellers for a time. "A-Team," with "Mr. T.," was so popular with kids at night that it was made into a Saturday morning cartoon show so the kids could see "Mr. T." twice a week, and in two different forms.

THE BEST MEDIA MIX

Obviously, if the television exposure given a property can be expanded with other media, so much the better. The value and appeal of the property will increase proportionately with the percentage of the target market made aware of it. The broader and more frequent this exposure, the better. Also, the faster the exposure is achieved, the sooner products achieve their secondary value.

There are instances in which a property can go beyond exposure on television. Movies are next best, then comic strips and comic magazines. The products themselves and their sales promotion, advertising, and merchandising at point of sale become a medium in themselves. In recent years, greeting cards have become an important medium. American Greet-

Fred Flintstone and his pal Barney Rubble with their kids Pebbles and Bamm Bamm played on prime-time television from 1960 to 1966. Children used the show as an excuse to stay up till 9:00 on Friday nights. Ideal Toys' Pebbles doll, Post Cereal's Pebbles, and nearly 3000 other items have made the Flintstones one of the all-time licensing hits. (Copyright 1986 Hanna-Barbera Productions, Inc. All rights reserved.)

ings and Hallmark have become vital factors in the licensing mix. But the conclusions one might reach regarding adequate media exposure are:

1. Hit movies alone seldom make great licensing properties. Exceptions are the blockbusters that usually create merchandise for one hot season.

2. Television one-shots (specials) or Saturday morning children's shows do not reach enough children often enough to make a program or a character popular with a vast number of children, however, they can function as important vehicles to sell licensed merchandise to the trade.

3. Syndicated shows and prime-time shows reaching a vast number of homes and children under 12 with a frequency

of at least once a week are the greatest creators of characters and ideas.

Guidelines such as these may seem so hard and fast they appear dogmatic. One quickly distrusts inflexible rules and questions their validity. There definitely are some exceptions, especially in recent years.

The Odd Case of "Sesame Street"

One such exception that comes to mind is the success of "Sesame Street" as a licensed property. After all, this is a commercial-free children's show that runs only on public television! This interesting exception reflects several important factors. In its earliest days (1969-70), the show ran as many as 18 times per week in most major markets (a fantastic frequency figure for a TV show). While the viewing of individual episodes was small, the cumulative audience per week was very high, as many as 9 million homes. In addition, by virtue of public sponsorship and the lack of competitive pressure, the show has remained on the air to the present.

This constant hammering away at a particular audience made it an excellent source of licensed merchandise for preschool children. Manufacturers of preschool products have "Sesame Street" products as perennials and at the height of this property's licensing vogue, 62 "Sesame Street" products were represented in the J.C. Penney Christmas catalog. "Sesame Street" character licensing is now a $200 million business at wholesale and its imprint appears on more than 1,700 items. Big Bird is a big star!

The Right Kind of Character

Beyond the sheer bulk of exposure, heavy television tonnage alone is not an absolute guarantee that a character or an idea will take off with children. They either like it or they don't. But there do seem to be some characteristics that guarantee popularity more than others.

Easy and correct definition of the character is most important. The character must be—or become—an essential part of the American popular culture mainstream. While the character can relate to or be reminiscent of characters which have come before, he or she must be unique in some important way. Uniqueness is usually achieved by a difference in personality, design, graphic execution, story line, or identity. It is seldom achieved by what the character stands for or the values associated with the character. These characters are usually larger than life. They are super special and can often perform extraordinary feats.

The character or the environment in which the character lives must have an instant ring of familiarity. These characters must live in a world children want to enter and experience through fantasy. The greater the appeal of the fantasy, the more times children want to experience this world. This really means repeated viewing.

The audience, particularly children, but preferably adults and children, must feel at home with the character. They must understand the character easily and what the character represents.

Original characters seem to work best. They are like annuities, forever generating revenue as new generations of children discover them. Joe Barbera, who with Bill Hanna created "Tom and Jerry," "Yogi Bear," "Huckleberry Hound," "The Flintstones," and "Scooby Doo," says that for a character to last "it must in some way represent the expression of an original vision, and not just exploit a passing fad. The characters must be individuals with recognizable human traits. They must touch a chord of familiarity among those watching."

Just as an aside, many programming properties are now being designed more for their merchandising potential than for their pure entertainment value, and are starting to depart from the single character concept. Many of these exploitative shows now contain numerous characters for the obvious reason that this creates multiple purchases by the consumer, rather than the single purchase of a single popular character. In addition, these shows include many more gadgets, gimmicks, hardware, and vehicles—the stuff of which kids products are made. And while many of the most famous characters of all time have been nonhuman, we are beginning to see many more programs and motion pictures in which humans are *mixed* with non-humans such as animals, aliens, and robots. These characters translate into toy products more easily than do human characters.

If it were possible, the marketing thinkers providing the input to television and movie creators would include both male and female heroes in every show. They know the sexes have distinct preferences for the characters they admire and love to see. Boys generally like male heroes; girls like both male and female characters.

MICKEY MOUSE: THE GREATEST SALESMAN OF THEM ALL

History shows us that Mickey Mouse is the greatest licensable character there has ever been. He has become the key figure in America's popular iconography. Mickey Mouse has the unique distinction of appealing to both sexes (though Walt Disney made sure to hedge his bet by including Minnie). Mickey Mouse also represents one of the purest comic-hero types seen in children's entertainment. Though Mickey has been in many different roles throughout his career, he has always been seen as the perfect American. He is 100 percent predictable as the nice guy, who, despite some occasional human failings, always opposes and conquers the forces of evil.

Mickey has what all great licensable characters have: the ability to endure and appeal to successive generations of children. The first Mickey Mouse products sold well to adults and children in the early '30s. Mickey's identity was known solely through the cartoon shorts shown in the movie theaters. Later, with comic books added, Mickey Mouse products did well through the '40s and into the '50s. The biggest boom came with the appearance of "The Mickey Mouse Club" on television. Mattel's "Mousegetars" were one of their all-time best selling products. What child could resist a "Mouseketeer" hat replete with Mickey's prominent ears? Even today, young children can't wait to visit Disneyland to see the real Mickey Mouse. Mickey remains the mainstay of the Disney empire.

Aside from being a unique figure, Mickey has played many different hero roles. His character is, generally speaking, closely related to the type of hero who traditionally has had the most appeal to boys. He has a long and rich tradition that can be traced back over 100 years in the United States.

The Noble Savage

Perhaps the root form for this type of American hero can be found in the Indian tales of James Fenimore Cooper, written in the early 1800s and read by almost every subsequent generation. He is *the most important* hero-type in American culture. The hero in Cooper's books is known by a number of names, Natty Bumpo, Deerslayer, Hawkeye, and Leatherstocking to name a few. Whatever name you remember him by, he is still the same hero. He is the outdoorsman who fights against the forces of evil. We know little of his origins or how he came by his profound knowledge of the woods and of weapons, but we know he is an expert with a gun and a knife. He is an excellent tracker and knows the Indians and their ways. Most importantly, he is a peaceable sort and doesn't look for trouble.

The Indians respect and admire him. In some stories he even appears with an Indian sidekick. He has little interaction with women, though women admire him from afar. In most of the stories he appears on the scene at the time of trouble and ultimately solves the problem with a violent solution. Negotiation is not his strong suit. The problem solved, he then takes off for uncharted territory.

Does he sound familiar? Of course, he does! By the time a child is eight years old he has already seen dozens of examples of this hero-type because his story is in the marrow of the American bone. He is part of our country's myth and folklore. We know him as well as anyone in our families. He has been the model for countless millions of American boys. We recognize him instantly. His morals are clear; his values are plain; his skills are obvious. A convenient label for him is the *noble savage*.

Even if you've never read Cooper or even heard of *The Last of the Mohicans,* there is a value in identifying him as the root form of the American hero because he pops up time and again in children's entertainment. You can recognize him in the various legends of Daniel Boone, Davy Crockett, Kit Carson, Jim Bridger, and a score of lesser known frontiersmen. Every one of these men had their day on prime-time television appealing to the youngsters of that generation, but perhaps the most merchandisable of them all was Davy Crockett.

DAVY CROCKETT

The best of the 1954 television season was a trilogy of Davy Crockett shows produced by Walt Disney as part of the Frontierland section on the "Disneyland" show. Originally, Disney's idea was to replace the hero over and over again with additional shows on American folk heroes, but he never got past Davy Crockett.

He never had to. Davy Crockett became a licensing gold mine. You may remember the song, "The Ballad of Davy Crockett." In sheet music alone the song sold three-quarters of a million copies. In record form, "The Ballad of Davy Crockett" sold more than 10 million copies in the United States, four million of which were twenty-five cent records, the type most commonly bought for or by children. By June 1955, about six months after the first Davy Crockett show was shown on television, more than $100 million worth of Davy Crockett character merchandise had been sold, with coonskin caps being far and away the most popular of the hundreds of different Davy Crockett items.

The Davy Crockett coonskin cap was an early example of a merchandising phenomenon that would repeat itself many times in years to come.

Six months after the first Davy Crockett show aired on television, more than $100 million worth of Davy Crockett character merchandise was sold, coonskin caps being far and away the most popular. (Copyright © 1955 The Walt Disney Company)

Although millions of caps sold very quickly because of the widespread fad with children, retailers ended up being stuck with storehouses full of merchandise. The reaction to fad items such as these is so great it seems there will be no end to the rush to buy. The manufacturer overproduces, the retailer overstocks, and the fad dies suddenly when the market is saturated. The amount of excess merchandise is tremendous and, unless they have been very cautious, the large retailers end up discounting the merchandise by heavy percentages or dumping it at a severe loss.

Market saturation, then, is one of the pitfalls of selling fad merchandise to youngsters and history has repeated itself dozens of times since then with the same phenomenon. In recent years, so-called adult toys have experienced similar disasters. Big important companies have gone broke. It happened with calculators, digital watches, and most recently with electronic games on which companies like Mattel, Atari, and Texas Instruments experienced losses mounting into the hundreds of millions of dollars. Even the most sophisticated marketers have difficulty forecasting the life span of a successful fad product.

The frontier hero brought to television has done reasonably well, but not even he has succeeded in every case. In the late '70s, CBS introduced "Young Daniel Boone" as a frontier adventure series in prime time at 8:00 P.M. Long before the series was on the air almost a dozen manufacturers signed up to make Daniel Boone merchandise. It was a poor guess this time. The show was quickly cancelled when it couldn't get an audience.

Other Cowboys

The frontiersman hero, both in fiction and reality, was only a model for the cowboys to come. In our stories of the Old West the legendary noble savage appears as a lawman or a gunfighter. While many stories were drawn from the real lives of these men, we know enough about them to recognize that some were considerably less than heroes. The exploits and adventures of William "Buffalo Bill" Cody, Wild Bill Hickock, and Wyatt Earp as told by author Ned Buntline in his stories of the Old West, were the beginnings of many myths that sprang up about these men. Celebrated in song and story, books and movies, these famous gunmen too found their way to television and became the prototype Western hero we recognize today. We see the noble savage myth perpetuated over and over throughout the media so that by the time a child is nine years old, he or she understands and relates to this particular hero instantly, no matter what name he carries or what form of environment he is found in.

The movies have had more popular versions of this hero than any other medium—from Bill Hart and Tom Mix to Buck Jones, Ken Maynard, and Hopalong Cassidy. Gene Autry and Roy Rogers were the kings of the "B" Westerns and each of them had a large following for their endless string of movies. The more artful Western films did a great deal to glorify and perpetuate the cowboy hero in movies like *Shane* with Alan Ladd, *High Noon* with Gary Cooper, and *Stagecoach,* plus countless other films featuring John Wayne.

Ralston cereals sponsored Tom Mix on the radio during the '30s and offered children a variety of licensed premiums. One of these was the Ralston Straight Shooter Manual telling about the real adventures of Tom Mix. (By permission of Ralston Purina Company)

Comics, radio, and television have also played a strong hand in establishing the noble savage myth in the American consciousness. Most of these treatments have been purer and simpler versions of the same hero in such fictional characters as the Lone Ranger and Red Ryder. Both of these Western knights, introduced over 50 years ago, always appeared with Indian sidekicks—direct and complete interpretations of Cooper's earlier noble savage characters. Interestingly enough, almost all of these Western heroes have had their merchandising heyday. As a child, my favorites were Tom Mix and the Lone Ranger.

TOM MIX

Tom Mix made some 180 films, but it was his radio show, starting in 1933, that captured the hearts of his younger fans. The radio program, sponsored by Ralston Cereals, probably offered the greatest variety of Tom Mix licensed premium rings, badges, and toys of any kids' hero from the '30s to the '50s. In addition to all the Horseshoe Nail Rings, Tom Mix Spurs, Compass Magnifying Glasses, postal-telegram sets, identification bracelets, decoder badges, and wooden six-shooters you could get if you were a Tom Mix Straight Shooter, you got a Straight Shooter manual telling you how great the real-life Tom Mix was. The manual told you Tom Mix had been a soldier of fortune with Teddy Roosevelt's Rough Riders in Cuba, that he had fought in the Boxer Rebellion in China, and the Boer War in South Africa. He was a cowboy, a sheriff, a U.S. Marshal, a Texas Ranger, a rodeo champion, and a movie star.

The Ralston Straight Shooter manual showed you the "Tom Mix Chart of Wounds," showing 12 bullet wounds and 47 bone fractures from movie stunts. A note on the chart indicates it did not show you his 22 knife wounds or the hole four inches square in his back caused by a dynamite explosion. Tom Mix was every boy's dream hero, a legendary godhead.

The truth was that Tom Mix was an old roué who ran through three wives and four million dollars. What's more, he had never left the country for any foreign wars; he only served as the town marshal in Dewey, Oklahoma, and as a prohibition agent in another small town. The legend and the dream had all been the work of advertising and publicity agents. Nevertheless, I wish I still had *the wooden model of this famous six-shooter*. It cost me a dime and a Ralston box top in 1938. It's worth about $40 in the nostalgia collector's market today.

THE LONE RANGER

The Lone Ranger was my other boyhood favorite. The Lone Ranger radio show began in 1932 and continues to this day in syndicated reruns. Even back in the '30s and '40s with the non-visual medium of radio, it would have been difficult to find a hero with so distinct and powerful an image as the Lone Ranger. He, above all, is one of the purest descendants of Cooper's noble savage.

Actually the idea for the Lone Ranger was based on Zorro, the

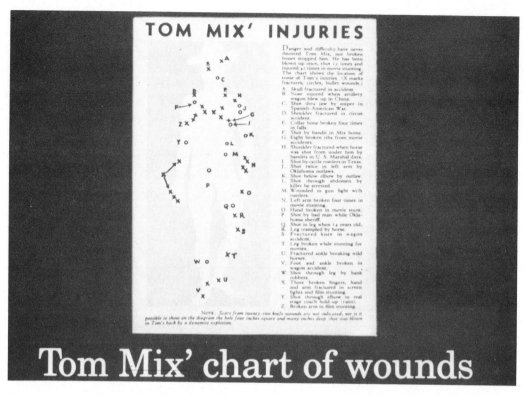

Tom Mix' chart of wounds

The Ralston Straight Shooter Manual showed the Tom Mix Chart of Wounds showing 12 bullet wounds and 47 bone fractures from movie stunts. A note on the chart indicates that it does not show 22 knife wounds nor the four-inch square wound that was caused by a dynamite explosion. (By permission of Ralston Purina Company)

masked avenger of Old California created by novelist Johnston McCulley in 1919. Conceived by a young writer named Fran Striker as an avenging angel of justice, the Lone Ranger radio show had many regional sponsors originally (mostly bread companies). Eventually the show was taken over by General Mills in the '40s. They solicited box tops from Kix, Cheerios, and Wheaties in exchange for a silver bullet ring and a ring topped with the Lone Ranger's six shooter. Toy stores abounded with Lone Ranger merchandise and plenty of it can still be found today. Naturally it sells best where youngsters have had an opportunity to see the Lone Ranger reruns on local television.

ZORRO

While television has held an entire host of Western heroes, from Marshal Matt Dillon of "Gunsmoke," to the three stars of "Maverick," and Paladin of "Have Gun Will Travel" fame, one of the most successful of the heroes from a merchandising point of view was "Zorro."

This show, produced by Walt Disney, was a half-hour, once-a-week series that ran for two years (1957-59). The series consisted of 39 episodes based on the fictional book that inspired the Lone Ranger and a host of heroes to come.

Guy Williams played the part of Zorro in the series. The Zorro character was already known to most adults through motion pictures in which two great film stars, Douglas Fairbanks and Tyrone Power, played the role. The Zorro stories were written about the period in the early 1800s when Spanish California was ruled by military dictatorship. Zorro had a dual identity as a spineless intellectual during the day and a masked avenger at night (shades of Superman and Batman) that enabled him "to aid the oppressed and punish the unjust." Williams quickly became one of the most popular television personalities in the United States. The "Zorro" show enjoyed one of the highest ratings ever recorded at the time and reportedly reached 35 million viewers each week during its two-year run.

The show's instant popularity and the enthusiastic reception given this type of hero enabled the Disney organization to license hundreds of pieces of merchandise carrying the picture of Zorro, not to mention the hats, masks, swords, and capes associated with the hero's familiar costume.

THE COPS AND ROBBERS

As the Western shows began to cancel one another out, American television tastes turned to the cops and robbers show. The licensed merchandise changed with the new trend, but the heroes did not. The sheriff's star became a badge and the cowboy chaps became street clothes as television ushered in a parade of cops, detectives, and private investigators. Old familiar standbys like Dick Tracy were transformed into animation for the younger set. Dick Tracy had not been seen since the period between 1937 and 1947, when kiddies saw him on live-action Saturday matinee serials and in the eight feature films released during that time. Today the Gold Key Entertainment Company has the rights to those films and has released them again.

Quaker Oats cereal sponsored Dick Tracy on the radio and started the Dick Tracy Secret Service Patrol. A bronze sergeant's badge cost five box tops, a silver lieutenant's badge seven, and a gold captain's 15. For the ultimate rank of Inspector-General, you had to recruit a new recruit for the Patrol. Tracy, when translated to animated television, did not change

Dick Tracy was one of the most popular characters in the cops and robbers genre. He started in the comics, then went on radio, and was later converted to an animated television show. Quaker Oats cereal sponsored the radio show and the Dick Tracy Secret Service Patrol. You sent in box tops to win various badges and the official watch. (Reprinted by permission: Tribune Media Services)

character. Other cop or private eye heroes like Jack Webb in "Dragnet," and all the other old standbys were much the same. The Western sheriffs had merely changed costumes. They were the same noble savages punishing the bad guys, with the Indian sidekick transformed into a buddy or a boy as exemplified by Dick Tracy and Junior.

Actually the crime show form, while watched and adored by millions of kids, for some reason never became an important merchandising concept. Perhaps "Dragnet," "Naked City," "Kojak," and "Starsky and Hutch" were all too real and too close to the bone to create a child's fantasy of the superhero.

THE SUPERSPY

The same hero, however, when cast as an international superspy, fired the imagination. Such characters as James Bond and "The Man from U.N.C.L.E.," because of their fantastic exploits and avalanche of far out gear, became larger-than-life figures and consequently, more heroic in the traditional sense. The weaponry and modes of transportation used by these international spies gave the toy designers and merchandise exploiters richer opportunities to intrigue boys with new play patterns.

James Bond might be called the logical and ultimate extension of the realistic modern superhero. He attains as far as we can go in the realm of realism. As Tom Wolfe pointed out, the only difference between James Bond and the Lone Ranger is that he doesn't leave a silver bullet when the episode is over—he fills out a report in triplicate.

THE SUPERHERO

Somewhere along the line our need for fantasy required the development of heroes who pushed beyond the boundaries of urban realism. Our myth of Cooper's noble savage frontiersman had to be translated into newer, neo-scientific urban form. Hence, we have Superman and a whole galaxy of other bizarre superheroes.

Superman made his debut in the June 1938 issue of Action Comics, and became one of the most popular formulas in mass literature. The whole concept of *Super* and its function in our lives has become a living melodrama in the Western world. As P. Wyndham Lewis wrote at the time, this romantic idea became "the gospel of action." The musket of the frontier was now traded in for speed faster than a speeding bullet and the incredible agility to leap tall buildings. The keen eye of the marksman and tracker was swapped for "X-Ray vision," the ability to see through walls and for tremendous distances. Defying all the laws of physics, it is only natural the mystical figure of superman should be above mere justice. Helpless police constantly call on him for assistance.

Appropriately, Superman was created by two young men still in their teens, Jerry Siegel and Joe Schuster. But they owe a debt to some previous fictional characters. Physically and mentally, Superman is a lot like Doc Savage, a hero of the pulp magazines who was referred to as a "superman." In his costume, he resembles Lee Falk's comic strip hero, the Phantom, and the idea of a double identity can be traced back to Zorro.

COPYRIGHT © DC COMICS INC. 1982

Superman has been a popular superhero since 1938. His latest movies and more than 100 licensors assure he will go on being a super businessman for many more years. (Copyright DC Comics Inc. 1982)

The instant success of Superman brought forth a potent team of impersonators, all the same type of muscular hero but with different sets of fantastic abilities. All of them—Batman, Captain Marvel, Captain America, Plastic Man, The Flash, Spider Man, even a sub-sister, Wonder Woman, live in a crime-threatened America. Each, as seen in the comics and later in movies and television, spends his or her life fighting the corrupt villains who threaten society. Problem after problem is soloved in an orgy of muscularity.

The Indian sidekick, once a staple of the frontiersman or Western hero story, is traded in for a boy. Batman had his ward, Robin; Captain America has his boy companion, Bucky; and the Marvel family, Captain Marvel Jr., who eventually got his own comic book. Some social commentators have pointed out the use of the boy companion has always seemed an awkward relationship. Because the boys are not sons or nephews, it is a difficult companionship to describe in conventional juvenile story terms. Due to the homosexual implications, the relationship has always been left vague. How many of us can even remember how Bucky is related to Captain America? Strange as these relationships seem, they are enormously helpful in creating the fantasy of the hero in young minds. A young

DC COMICS INC. **COPYRIGHT © 1982**

The sidekick, once the staple of the frontiersman or the western hero, has more recently been traded in for a boy. Witness Batman and his ward, Robin. (Copyright DC Comics Inc. 1982)

superhero fan cannot always make the fantasy leap of pretending to be his favorite superhero. It is easier to imagine oneself as the boy in the relationship—the close friend of the hero and the ally in adventures. Inevitably the younger, less skilled companion occasionally helps the hero out of a jam, and that's the greatest thrill of all. Beyond that, when heroic actions are seen through the eyes of a boy, deeds appear even more wondrous. A boy's viewpoint was skillfully presented in the movie *Shane*. Alan Ladd's fistfights and gunfights are all seen through the eyes of the boy played by Brandon de Wilde. He watches his hero's every move, wide-eyed and filled with admiration.

Superman, Batman and Robin, Spider Man, and Wonder Woman were all turned into television shows since their comic book days. And all of them became merchandising classics. Superman, far from retirement, has bounded to new heights in his licensing career on the strength of several recent motion pictures, each budgeted at more than $25 million. The first was released in the summer of 1978, but the promotion drums had already begun beating loudly. More than 100 Superman licensers signed up long before the movie opened. Superman is destined to be a super businessman for many more years.

TARZAN

Cowboys, cops, and caped crimefighters are not the only occupations of the lineage of heroes in the noble savage tradition. Locations and environments can easily be switched depending upon the author's interest. Retaining the formula for the hero, Edgar Rice Burroughs made a perfect switch in 1914 with his first movie, *Tarzan of the Apes*. Tarzan has, for years, been one of the most memorable, if not merchantable, American heroes.

Tarzan, the offspring of Lord and Lady Greystoke, follows the same pattern of mysterious origins. Through a story convention, he grows up in the African jungle protected by a she-ape from wild creatures and hostile natives. Self-educated in the lore of the jungle and possessing superhuman strength and skills, he befriends the good creatures and protects them against the forces of evil.

The Tarzan legend is so simple, so quickly understood by all generations, it has stood the test of time in many forms—the 21 original novels by Burroughs, comic strips and comic books, a daily radio serial, movies, and television. The movies did the most to popularize the Tarzan character, providing him with all the familiar formulas, including a female companion and the boy sidekick, to make the stories in tune with the mainstream American culture hero of the day.

Though Tarzan probably represents the purest example of the noble savage character and has had tremendous exposure over the years, he has not proved to be much of a gold mine for the merchandise makers. After all, how much can you do with a leopardskin loincloth and a rubber knife? Beyond that, the visual image of Tarzan is unclear. We have seen him in comic strip illustrations, in the movies played by Lex Barker and Johnny Weismuller, and a host of other lesser known players. Even though his image seems to persist as Johnny Weissmuller (at least to my generation) it is doubtful the youngsters of today recognize Tarzan as any one particular face. The latest Tarzan movies have done nothing to help the situation. In one he is overshadowed by Bo Derek in sexy garb, and *Greystoke,* the newest version of Tarzan, is a psychodrama far more appealing to adults.

THE NOBLE SAVAGE IN SPACE

The '70s and '80s have not produced any new hero types of consequence. We came full circle with another superman impersonator in "The Six Million Dollar Man." This popular nighttime show brought the Superman formula up-to-date in neo-scientific terms and ironically paved the way for a new wave of popularity for the *original* Superman character. In the meantime, "Six Million Dollar Man" merchandise was very lucrative in the marketplace. The male action figure of Lee Majors alone sold in the millions.

Neo-scientific fantasy, science fiction, and the fantasies of other worlds have become and will continue to be the grist for new television shows and movies for many years to come. *Star Wars* was only the tip of the iceberg. Luke Skywalker comes right out of the same mold as his heroic antecedents, but curiously he is not nearly as well developed as some of the robot-like characters in the film.

Luke, of course, was not the first noble savage in space. He has a long tradition. Buck Rogers was introduced in a comic strip on January 7, 1929 and was a popular comic character until 1967. During that period Buck Rogers was translated into 18 languages and appeared in more than 450 newspapers. When *Star Wars* appeared, owners of the Buck Rogers rights ran a trade ad headlined, "*Star Wars* owes it all to Buck Rogers."

While all of Buck Rogers adventures were marked by the same wild conglomeration of technological prophecy we see in *Star Wars,* Buck was a hero in the traditional mold. His mission was to save the universe from such archvillains as Killer Kane and the slinky Ardala, and he was constantly zapping them with cosmic weapons like Rocket Pistols.

Of course, Rocket Pistols were turned into licensed merchandise and when Macy's department store advertised the toy version of Buck Rogers' Disintegrator Guns, the next morning a line of 20,000 people, a third of a mile long, awaited the store's opening. If you could find one of those pistols today, it would cost you upwards of 45 dollars.

The kids of today experienced Buck Rogers when Universal Studios created a new television series released in 1978. For several seasons, it was the most popular nighttime show for boys. Strangely enough, and I suspect it is because Universal has not been a visionary or astute licensor, Buck Rogers merchandise did not do well in the marketplace.

The original success of Buck Rogers brought forth another equally popular imitator. When the planet Mongo threatened to collide with Earth in 1934, a Yale-bred polo player named Flash Gordon and a beautiful girl named Dale Arden were kidnapped and taken aboard the rocket of the crazed Hans Zarkov. Based on this idea, cartoonist Alex Raymond launched Flash Gordon, first in the comic strips, then in Big Little Books, and eventually on the screen. Olympic swimming star Buster Crabbe played Flash in the movies in traditional noble savage form, saving the Earth from the evil doings of Ming the Merciless. The values of the frontier were translated to the Yale polo field by cartoonist Raymond and eventually to a War of the Worlds. Raymond said, "This was a Tournament of Death, but it was still to be fought by heroes imbued with the ideals of sportsmanship and fair play."

Flash Gordon returned in a major movie in the fall of 1978 produced by Dino de Laurentiis. In addition, the old Flash Gordon movie serials were syndicated and some hundreds of tie-in products briefly appeared in the marketplace. But like the return of Buck Rogers, the merchandising did not take off.

More recent versions of the American noble savage hero have appeared in hybrid forms, but are still direct descendants of the comic strips. Indiana Jones is a combination of Jungle Jim, the Phantom, and Flash Gordon. He-Man and Conan are simply Superman in other worlds. And Mr. T is an inner-city, urban, black version of the superhero crimefighter in a superpunk getup, an obvious throwback to the comic strips.

MICKEY MOUSE: HIS DESCENDANTS AND HIS IMITATORS

It is abundantly clear the American culture superhero mainstream moves in a fairly direct line from Deerslayer to Dick Tracy, from Superman to "Six Million Dollar Man," into space and time, then back again to the city streets endlessly battling the forces of evil. One might well ask how we can account for the success of Mickey Mouse and his hundreds of imitators who obviously depart from the mainstream tradition. What is the relationship?

Actually, the departure is not so great as one might imagine. The only real difference between the original Mickey Mouse and the noble savage hero is that Mickey is good for laughs. Mickey Mouse, Yogi Bear, Huckleberry Hound, and the rest are still true-blue, staunch Americans, morally opposed to bad guys and wrongdoers. Each of them solves problems by more or less violent solutions.

Mickey was introduced in a barnyard environment in his first strip in January 1930, then quickly moved to a desert island loaded with cannibals. Early in Mickey's career he constantly fought with archvillains like Sylvester Shyster, a crooked lawyer "who'd stick a knife in your back" and the fiendish, but dumb, Pegleg Pete. The real difference between Mickey, the animated comic hero to follow, and the classical hero is that Mickey and his friends are not so deadly serious as the mainstream types. They make a mistake now and then, creating a laugh. In addition to possessing heroic attributes they are buffoons and the subjects of tall tales. They are larger than life and they are unique.

The ancestor for this type of comic hero can be found in American frontier literature. He exists as Paul Bunyan, as Mike Fink, the Riverboat man, and in the stories of Pecos Bill. Later we find the same character more purely expressed in the comic strips as Joe Palooka, L'il Abner, and Popeye. Of these characters, only Popeye has been brought to the screen successfully. In the early days of television, the old Popeye theatrical cartoon became material for the hottest local kid shows.

There has never been a greater salesman than Mickey Mouse. To get some idea of the tremendous scope of products "sold by Mickey Mouse," one must read *Disneyana*, a 385-page work by Cecil Munsey. The book catalogs and describes the literally thousands of products sold by Mickey and other Disney characters over the past 50 years. By the mid 1930s, according to Munsey, Mickey was "the best known and most popular international figure of the day." The audience, composed of 20 million daily readers of 330 newspapers in which Mickey appeared, also saw him in cartoons in more than 10,000 theatres in the United States alone. General Foods spent $1.5 million to acquire the rights to put Mickey's

Donald Duck is typical of Mickey Mouse's friends. They aren't as serious as mainstream hero characters even though they are larger than life. They make mistakes and make you laugh. (Copyright © The Walt Disney Company)

Mickey Mouse has the advantage of appealing to both sexes, though Walt Disney made sure to hedge his bet by including Minnie. (Copyright © The Walt Disney Company)

Yogi Bear and Huckleberry Hound as comic heros are literary descendants of Mickey Mouse. Huck was an easygoing, homespun guy from Tennessee; and Yogi was a "smarter than the average bear" who reminded you of Art Carney's sewer-engineer, Ed Norton. These characters and others launched Hanna-Barbera's multimillion dollar licensing business. (Copyright 1983 Hanna-Barbera Productions, Inc. All rights reserved.)

Porky Pig and Tweety are two of the many Warner Brothers Looney Tunes characters that generate retail sales of more than $100 million every year. While their television exposure is minimal, they remain classics in the comic character genre. (Copyright Warner Bros. Inc. 1966)

name on Post toasties; Cartier sold Mickey Mouse charms and bracelets in gold and platinum for as much as $1,250. Whatever products Mickey endorsed, for children or adults, sold very well.

One of Mickey's most spectacular merchandising successes was his association with Lionel, the toy train company. In May 1934, Lionel went into receivership with liquid assets of $62,000 and liabilities amounting to $296,000. In July, Lionel came out with a Mickey Mouse licensed handcar toy with a 27 inch circle of track. It sold for $1 a set. In four months, they sold 253,000 sets. The success allowed Lionel to borrow enough money from the banks to save the company from bankruptcy.

COMIC HEROES

With the exception of Mickey Mouse, the farther a character strays from the mainstream hero attributes, the less his or her drawing power in merchandising terms. When the character becomes more comic and less heroic, even if his popularity is tremendous, he somehow loses his merchandising force. As a straight comic, a character can be loved and laughed at, but does not necessarily become part of a child's fantasy. If we view the historic development of the merchandising hero over the past 50 years, it is evidently easier for boys to play cowboys and Indians, cops and robbers, or even space commandos or swords and sorcery than it is to play clowns and comics. Animated heros like Porky Pig and Bugs Bunny seem like by-products of the Hollywood studio dream factory, rather than the colossal superstars of merchandising. Nevertheless, they are not to be ignored as sales stimulators. Licensing Corporation of America claims the 20 main Warner Bros. Looney Tunes characters generate retail sales of over $100 million annually in goods and services. While children seldom aspire to become a clown or a funny character, they love them all the same and remember them. Children recognize their favorites instantly and will buy replicas of them or merchandise from them when the clown turns salesman. McDonald's could have done no better when creating Ronald McDonald as its spokesman to children. And Bozo the Clown has been around for years as a children's favorite.

ATHLETES

Given children's apparent need for fantasies of power and success, it is a little odd that famous athletes have not emerged as stronger merchandising images. In recent years it appears that only O.J. Simpson is well-known and liked by the children's mass audience. At this time there is no one overwhelmingly famous baseball player, basketball player, or Olympic athlete, although several star athletes manage to sell some merchandise. Even Muhammad Ali was not a sensational hit as a boy's male action figure.

One can hardly discuss the athlete heroes of recent times without touching on another strange, but interesting phenomenon—Evel Knievel. He defies classification except as a daredevil. But, his larger-than-life exploits made him a fantastic merchandising freak. He had reasonably strong television exposure for his stunts, but if one were to measure the children's audience, the commercials selling Evel Knievel motorcycle toys probably had more reach and frequency than any coverage of his real-life activities.

VILLAINS AND MONSTERS

Villains have never existed independently of heroes or done well as licensed characters; yet, there is a certain adoration children have for comic villains in the form of monsters. Children love monsters and they love to see them undone. They are not the least bit afraid as long as the monsters are recognizable and predictable in their downfall. There are only a few monsters that are recognized by all generations. First and foremost are Frankenstein's monster and Dracula. Is there a child who cannot imitate Frankenstein's monster's walk or the Transylvanian accent of the Vampire as played by Bela Lugosi? King Kong is also well-known. So is Godzilla, who after 17 films is about to experience a revival. These monsters have always been merchandising favorites because their exposure is continual in a multitude of forms. It would take a tremendous prime-time show with weekly exposure to create another monster as famous as any of these.

THE CRITERIA FOR GIRL'S HEROINES

All of the observations made thus far about American mainstream culture heroes concern only boys' favorites. If history is any guide, the pattern points the way for future favorites as well. For the merchandise maker and licenser, the mainstream noble savage hero should continue to be a sure bet, as should some of the comic heroes. Other formulas are considerably more risky. And, without question, the same formulas do not apply to girls' heroes and heroines or the licensed characters for girl's merchandise.

Girl's heroes and heroines are far more difficult to define. The picture is not nearly as clear, perhaps because fewer of them have become legendary. There are fewer heroines to analyze for common patterns. Yet, if one could trace a pure line of girl's heroines, the most prevalent and successful characters through time do have some common characteristics:

1. They are young, either children or girls, seldom women.

2. They are innocent. Feminine, but never sexual.

3. They are usually pretty, clever, and gifted.

4. They have high morals and exemplary behavior.

5. They are admired by adults as well as children.

These pristine creatures march through time with astonishing regularity. We know them as Cinderella, Alice in Wonderland, and Snow White. In the books and comic strips, radio serials, and films of yesteryear we recognize this innocent girl heroine as Rebecca of Sunnybrook Farm, Dorothy in *The Wizard of Oz,* Nancy Drew, and Raggedy Ann.

LITTLE ORPHAN ANNIE

During the '20s and '30s the leading heroine was Little Orphan Annie. When Little Orphan Annie first appeared in 1929, she seemed out of place on the funny pages for the simple reason she was rarely funny. Rather, cartoonist Harold Gray continuously sent his never-aging little red haired tyke and her dog Sandy to the aid of decent folks in jeopardy from treacherous foreigners and crimelords.

By 1930, Annie became "the Chatterbox with pretty auburn locks" when she went on the radio for the Wander Company, makers of Ovaltine. Ovaltine offered "Little Orphan Annie's very own Shake-Up Mug" for the aluminum seal from an Ovaltine can and ten cents. They sold millions. Annie's radio show also made popular a series of paper items like masks and talking stationery on which a likeness of Annie appeared to move her lips. Her biggest item was the famous decoding badge which was issued new every year from 1935 to 1940.

Annie is such a quintessential girls' heroine, one might well ask why she hasn't been brought to television with her own series. Perhaps we'll see that yet, but I'm certain the networks will have to be convinced the series can appeal to boys as well as girls. No programmer wants to reach only half the audience.

The moviemakers evidently did not have that same problem. The precedent setting popularity of *Snow White* and *Mary Poppins* evidently gave them the confidence to make a big budget version of *Annie* just a few years ago. In addition, there had been an enormously popular, long running Broadway show *Annie,* which the producers were certain was going to bring adults and families to the movie houses.

Little Orphan Annie has been a leading heroine for girls since 1929. First in the Sunday comics, then in radio, and more recently in a major motion picture, Annie is a quintessential innocent girl heroine. (Reprinted by permission: Tribune Media Services)

Both at the box office and as a licensed product, Annie was a disappointment. It simply was not the kind of film that children wanted to see over and over again.

From a character merchandising and promotion point of view I doubt if any film has ever been handled more adroitly. The prerelease publicity was enormous. To sell the licensing rights, Columbia hired an ex-Mattel marketer named Joe Whittaker. Few people understand all the moves as well as Whittaker. He had been an integral part of the Barbie, Hot Wheels, Flipper, and G.I. Joe phenomena. The problem, in retrospect, was that Whittaker probably did too good a job attracting and selling the Annie license to manufacturers. He sold over 100 different licenses to almost as many different companies. Every conceivable item which might have appealed to young girls jumped on the licensing bandwagon for this potentially blockbusting movie. But few items other than doll replicas of Annie sold very well. Perhaps there was too much Annie merchandise on

Shirley Temple was the innocent girl heroine of the '30s. The Ideal Toy Company manufactured Shirley Temple dolls and sold 6 million of them priced from $3.00 to $30.00 each. Every package had the star's name written in her own child's scrawl and there was an endless stream of costumes for the dolls that were replicas of her movie roles. (Courtesy, Viewmaster Ideal Group Inc.)

the market at one time. The limited appeal of the character was fractionalized into too many parts. Bernie Loomis, the man behind *Star Wars* toys, Strawberry Shortcake, and Care Bears said he did not think Annie was *toyetic,* a word he coined meaning: "after you've made the big dolls and the small dolls, what else can you do with her?"

While Annie was the perfect innocent girl heroine, she should not be mistaken for other heroines of the comic strips. She is not Tillie the Toiler, Ella Cinders, Dixie Dugan, Etta Kett, Brenda Starr, Blondie, or Betty Boop. Nor is she Fritzi Ritz, whose strip didn't become popular with children until its emphasis was switched to her niece Nancy. Little Orphan Annie was practically the only innocent girl heroine originated by the comics.

SHIRLEY TEMPLE

The other best known innocent girl heroine of the time was best personified by Shirley Temple. First seen in 1934 at the age of five in *Stand up and Cheer,* she became the child of the next decade. One of her many films was *Little Miss Marker. Time* magazine noted she might well have been called "Little Miss Mark-Up." She was one of Hollywood's top box office draws from 1935-1938, making an average of four pictures a year which grossed $5 million annually. Her royalties were enormous.

Shirley Temple dolls appeared, with doll clothes and accessories, soap, books, and ribbons. Shirley Temple as an eye rolling, Daddy's delight was the perfect innocent girl heroine—the little girl every other little girl wanted to be. The Ideal Toy Company, the manufacturer of Shirley Temple Dolls, sold six million doll replicas of her at $3 to $30 each. Every package had the star's name written in her own childish scrawl and there was an endless string of costumes for the dolls inspired by her movie roles.

DOROTHY

One of the roles originally planned for Shirley Temple was Dorothy in the MGM version of *The Wizard of Oz*. While the Oz books have been published steadily since 1900 and their innumerable editions have outsold all other American children's books, the 1939 MGM movie did more to popularize the familiar heroine of Dorothy and the wonderful characters from Oz than any treatment preceding it. The early Oz books spawned a few Oz novelties—games, puzzles, and unattractive stuffed dolls—but the 1939 movie inspired a great deal more merchandise, such as Oz dolls in various sizes, Oz charm bracelets, pencil boxes, coloring books, games, and phonograph records. By 1940, when the MGM film played out its last bookings, most of the merchandising came to a halt. Strangely enough, in 1956 the copyright on *The Wizard of Oz* expired and the story and its characters went into public domain. MGM only controlled the license to their film version of the story and consequently the property has since been kicked about by everybody with no control of the integrity of the characters.

BARBIE

After 1939, no other character for girls was as popular as Dorothy until 1958. In that year Mattel introduced a new kind of doll destined to become the most popular licensed female character for the next 20 years. The doll's name was Barbie and she was presented on television as the ultimate extension of the innocent girl heroine. For little girls seeing her commercials, Barbie became the most famous teenage fashion model in

They can't cancel Barbie.

Barbie is the sales-leading-lady who rules the U.S. fashion doll market with her stable profit-making personality.

This Mattel trade ad makes the point to the toy industry that unlike most licensed characters coming out of television shows, Barbie goes on and on through the exposure of her television commercials alone. (Courtesy, Mattel Inc.)

the world. Barbie lovers joined a worldwide fan club and sent her over 10,000 letters per week—more than any other television or movie celebrity, except Shirley Temple.

Hundreds of television commercials have dramatized Barbie over the past years and her name has become a household word. Almost 100 other manufacturers have made use of her popularity, licensing her name from Mattel for their merchandise. It is estimated that more than $1 billion worth of Barbie merchandise has been sold at retail since she was launched on the tube. To the merchandising world, Barbie is a doll, the multi-million dollar leader in the category of fashion dolls. But to little girls, Barbie is a real Superstar, a never-aging glamorous teenager who goes on exciting adventures with her boyfriend Ken and her other friends.

Barbie was the first doll with breasts and a realistic figure, but she remains in the mold of the innocent girl heroine. She appears to be going on forever, or at least as long as her television exposure stays at its current level. A few years ago, Barbie's championship as a licensed character for

Gershan Legnan once described Wonder Woman as having "the drum majorette patriotism of starspangled panties and spread-eagled breasts." It's difficult to determine whether she appeals to girls or boys. (Copyright DC Comics Inc. 1982)

girls was challenged by Farrah Fawcett-Majors. While not exactly a classic innocent girl, Farrah was not far from it. Some observers commented that Farrah Fawcett was just Barbie in the flesh. No other television heroines of the '70s emerged from television to take Barbie's place, although there were some brief vogues worth mentioning.

Musical stars like Cher and Marie Osmond had short spurts of popularity, and some heroines arose as counterparts to the male noble savage image. Descendents from Wonder Woman of the comic books and Sheena of the Jungle, active women heroines such as "Charlie's Angels" made a play for the imaginations of little girls of today. As the gap closed on the equality of the sexes, perhaps the formulas for girls favorites moved a little closer to the boys.

WONDER WOMAN

As with the male hero prototype, Wonder Woman and her sisters are all active super human forces fighting against evil—roping with her magic lasso, ripping the conning towers off submarines, and tying men up in knot after knot. *Wonder Woman* comic books were said to be aimed at young girls, but her lack of clothing certainly must have caught boys' eyes. Gershan Legman once described Wonder Woman as having "the drum majorette patriotism of star-spangled panties and spread-eagled breasts."

"She-Ra: Princess of Power," the heroine of a new animated show from Filmation, is a direct descendant of Wonder Woman. Instead of a magic lasso, she has The Sword of Protection when pitted against the Horde, a collection of evil villains. (Copyright 1985 Filmation Associates, Inc. Mattel, Inc.)

Certainly Wonder Woman, in her new form on television, the Bionic Woman, and Charlie's Angels received more than their share of attention from boys and even adult males. Consequently it is difficult to say whether or not this type of new heroine will have a lasting impact on the marketplace in terms of girls licensed products. At this writing we can now see the counterpart of "He-Man and the Masters of the Universe," a new series called "She-Ra: Princess of Power" from the same creators of "He-Man."

THE ROCK STARS

Equally difficult to predict is the lasting impact of the musical celebrity as a licensed character. The rock star is a recent development of the '50s and '60s and has become more of a teenage phenomenon than a commodity for children under 12. However, the counter-culture of the '60s has become so much a part of the mainstream that all of its artifacts and mannerisms—the long, unruly hair, the beads, the back-to-nature ga-ga, and the crunchy granola mentality—have all become commonplace for kids as well as everyone else.

With the '60s movement came the adulation of the musical star and a new hero for both boys and girls to imitate—the teenager. The girls adore the teenage stereotype as once popularized on television by Fonzie, of "Happy Days" and Vinnie Barberino, of "Welcome Back Kotter." The boys were too embarrassed to wear a Fonzie T-Shirt, but they were certainly more than overwhelmed with long hair, hot cars, surfing, rock music, and all the other associated jumble of graffiti that accompanied this new sub-culture and has become a part of American iconography.

Whether this new teenage world of rock stars and glitter will challenge the traditional merchandising heroes of old is open to question. Most assuredly, it is having its run now and is moving merchandise in astronomical numbers. The advent of such dance movies as *Saturday Night Fever* and *Flashdance* created a new look in young fashions. Michael Jackson's rock videos and personal appearances have made him the teen star of today. His one silver glove and pink socks have been widely imitated by teens. MTV, the Music Television network, has popularized a new video form that attracts older kids. Programmers are experimenting with cartoon versions of rock videos because they can't turn their backs on the latest phenomena. Whether or not this will become a form for children or will do any more in the market place than sell records and influence fashions is still very much unknown. There is no doubt that a large number of younger children under 12 are attracted to the menace and violence of the rock videos on MTV and its imitators like VH-1 and others. Whether they are identifying with the antiestablishment antics of the performers or merely identifying with the viewing habits of older teens is also unknown. No one has combined the MTV concept into hot selling children's merchandise.

THE CUTE CHARACTERS

No discussion of licensed characters would be complete without mentioning another subcategory from which popular characters occasionally emerge. This category, which I call "The Cute Characters," has more androgynous appeal. It is definitely skewed to little girls, but many of these characters also appeal to boys, albeit very young ones. The characters to which I am referring are childlike, actually like little children. Their root forms are in "The Katzenjammer Kids"; Henry, Nancy, and Sluggo of the comic strips; and in the early *Our Gang* movies and cartoons. Today you see them as Snoopy, Charlie Brown, and Lucy, and in more bizarre interpretations as the Smurfs, The Littles, the Care Bears, The Get Along Gang, and The Cabbage Patch Kids.

The one thing these characters have in common is they are "cute." They are usually small creatures and behave like children. Their appeal seems to be the paradox that though they are small, inexperienced, and unsophisticated, they are capable of simple profundities. They remind us of the simplest and best values.

LICENSING MADNESS

The competition for licensed dollars has become so fierce, so heated, that manufacturers are rushing headlong to put a licensed name on anything. Licensors, too, are growing indiscriminate about whom they will license or on what products they allow the licensed name to appear. Estimates for licensed product sales are about $40 billion. It is projected by the *Licensing Letter* that by 1990 sales will exceed $75 billion. In the last four years alone, licensed product sales have increased 400 percent.

The *Licensing Letter* also predicts that by 1990 there will be more than 2,000 individual licensed properties. What manufacturers are failing to notice is that only 10 of the 100 new properties introduced each year survive. Part of the reason for this phenomenon is that manufacturers were once content to allow popular licensed characters to emerge, catch as catch can, from the media. Movies and television were watched closely each season to see which shows or character personalities would take hold. Then the race would begin to capture and license the character with the most promise. Generally speaking, the rules and principles I have laid out, if used, could function as guidelines to decide which license to choose. Today, however, the industry has become so topsy-turvy, so unpredictable, no clear methodology serves to tell one what to bet on. And at 10 to 1 odds, the choices must be figured much more carefully.

Strawberry Shortcake was one of the biggest licensing hits the toy industry has ever seen. She was created by "Those guys from Cleveland," a creative group working for American Greeting cards and others. She was a concept before she became a toy, a greeting card, and hundreds of other licensed items. (Reprinted with permission of Those Characters from Cleveland, Inc.)

Perhaps the clearest cause for the licensing madness of recent years is the deliberate design and development of the licensed character as product preceding programming. In other words, it was reasoned that one could first design the character as a product, and product extensions, then write a television show starring this character, thereby reversing the traditional process. It had been done before by General Foods and Mattel with some success. The first time this technique was used to create a blockbuster was when General Mills and American Greetings Cards formed a partnership to create Strawberry Shortcake.

At the time, Bernie Loomis was at the head of the General Mills toy companies. He left Mattel to head up Kenner, General Mills largest toy division. At Kenner, Loomis had startled the toy industry with two notable licensing successes, "The Six Million Dollar Man" and *Star Wars*. These hits really kicked off today's licensing craze. Flushed with those successes and confident of his ability to spot and promote a winner, he jumped on Strawberry Shortcake. For a few years, he created one of the biggest hits the industry had ever seen. Hundreds of millions of dollars of Strawberry Shortcake merchandise was sold.

Strawberry Shortcake was a rather typical female heroine of the sort we described earlier. She was a cute little girl in a strawberry outfit designed to be used for juvenile stationery for American Greetings cards. Their creative group, "Those guys from Cleveland," invented the character. When the character was shown to Loomis as a licensing possibility for the General Mills toy companies, he quickly recognized its appeal. He also understood that there was no other hit product appealing to little girls at that time except for the perennial Barbie doll. The line of Strawberry Shortcake dolls, each of which came with its own scent, was actually a copy of Mattel's Kologne Kiddies of 10 years back, but the timing, the concept, and the promotion were exactly right for the marketplace.

The concept and product took off with comparatively little media exposure. To sell the line to the trade, Loomis had to promise some half-hour television specials and they, of course, were merely half-hour commercials for the product. The concept was also backed by an extensive print campaign showing all the various Strawberry Shortcake products in the market. Here was a case where the sheer number of products on the market became the most important media exposure of all.

THE LATEST CHARACTERS

Once this concept proved itself, it opened the floodgates. Mattel, along with my former associate, Eddie Smardan, had Filmation develop a series from their two-year-old toy line, He-Man and Masters of the Universe. G.I. Joe toys from Hasbro have been in and out of the market since the '60s. Today, G.I. Joe is part of an animated series in syndication, each episode a half-hour commercial for the product. Other animated specials and series are "The Gobots" and "Transformers," each successful toylines from Tonka and Hasbro. "The Care Bears," another Bernie Loomis production, duplicates almost exactly the pattern of introduction that made Strawberry Shortcake successful. Mattel has a second and a third entry with Rainbow Brite (done with Hallmark, who jumped on the bandwagon after American Greetings' successes) and "She-Ra," an animated series with a female heroine. The list goes on and on.

THE NEW SHAPE OF LICENSING

The licensing explosion and the half-hour commercial, while possibly a temporary condition, have created a new source for the characters and video literature of our children's culture. What was once the sole province of children's authors, comic strip artists, and film artists like Disney, Bill Hanna and Joe Barbera, and Jim Henson, has now become a creative outlet for toy and greeting card manufacturers.

Care Bears were almost a sequel to Strawberry Shortcake. Developed by the same people and promoted in the same formula, these bears with personalities became hot licensing characters. The Care Bears as products became popular enough to launch a successful movie for preschoolers—a rare case where the movie came after the product. (Reprinted with permission of Those Characters from Cleveland, Inc.)

Should this phenomena continue to grow, and it shows no sign of a slowdown, the new animation television programs will be dominated and commercially fueled by creations from toy companies. The outcries from ACT and other consumerist groups who claim these new shows are "over-commercialization" will not curb its momentum or growth. Only the marketplace will decide that.

Obviously, within a few seasons, too many licensed characters will crowd the marketplace. The glut will result in manufacturers and retailers growing weary of getting burned by bad guesses. The real control of the marketplace is in the hands of the licensing agents, who can decide which products enhance and prolong the life of their character and which will kill it off in a season or two.

There are only a few companies with the vision and foresight to do that. Most of the industry is filled with newcomers and exploiters who have charged in like miners to a gold rush.

The Importance of the Licensing Agent

Going back to my earlier principles, the successful licensed character must be sold by an aggressive but thoughtful licensing agent who maintains the integrity of the property. Each licensee must be chosen carefully. The licensing agent must consider what this manufacturer can do for the character and how the character fits into their line of products. The licensing agent must also maintain close watch over the product development and quality, and maintain strict marketing guidelines for each of the manufacturers. This type of control, originally employed by Disney, has totally broken down in today's exploding market.

The principles of licensing as originally created by Disney were really put into practice by the father of modern day licensing, a Kansas City advertising executive named Herman "Kay" Kamen. Starting his career as a hat salesman in 1918, he formed, with Streeter Blair, a Kansas City advertising agency in 1926 called Kamen-Blair. In 1932 Kamen made a long distance call to Walt Disney in Hollywood explaining he was interested in working with Disney character merchandise. After hearing a few of Kamen's innovative ideas, Disney invited him to Hollywood for further discussion.

Kamen signed his first contract with Disney in 1932. The contract called for Kamen to receive 40 percent of all monies received from licensees, and Disney 60 percent.

After six months, Kamen reported the sale of several million dollars worth of merchandise. In his first summer, Kamen facilitated the sale of 10 million Mickey Mouse ice cream cones and in 1933, he helped Ingersoll sell 900,000 Mickey Mouse watches and clocks. From 1933 to 1940 Ingersoll reports they sold approximately $5 million worth of Disney merchandise, representing a quarter of a million dollars in royalties. During that time, Macy's in New York sold as many as 11,000 Mickey Mouse watches in one day.

Kamen represented Disney until 1948. By that time his reports showed more than 2,000 articles bearing the imprint of the Disney characters were turned out and distributed by 150 firms in the United States and another 500 in Europe and the rest of the world. That same year Kamen was killed in an airplane crash. With his death came the end of an era, 17 years of innovative leadership in the character merchandising field.

At this time the Walt Disney Character Merchandising division was created. Today, it consists of 29 offices representing 72 countries. Retail sales of Disney products are estimated at more than $2 billion annually, worldwide. Disney items now number in the 8,000 range with 1,600 licenses worldwide.

The Need for Quality and Control

Disney continues to adhere to the principles of quality and control that they established from the start. Also following the high quality standard is The Children's Television Workshop with "Sesame Street" licensees, now a $200 million business. And so does Henson Associates in their licensing of the Muppets and Fraggle Rock, now estimated to be earning approximately $150 million annually. Other top people in the field are George Lucas, Licensing Corporation of America, DIC Merchandising, Stan Weston's Leisure Concepts, and, of course, the licensing arms of Hanna-Barbera and Filmation. These groups try to keep the industry professional and reasonably wholesome. They recognize that glutting the market with inferior merchandise will only result in killing the goose that provided so many golden eggs.

Manufacturer confidence is also an issue. With so many licensed products on the market, it is difficult to pick a hit. The character makers are using children's television indiscriminately, with no consideration for taste, quality, or even entertainment. The primary goal seems to be to get the product on the air, to expose the property to the kids to make it popular. Half-hour commercials are essential, in their mentality, along with the 30- and 60-second commercials.

It is my hope, through the foregoing examination, history, and analysis to establish a little reason, and bring some caution and order to an industry that is growing up too fast. With so much emphasis placed on licensing, children's television is taking a direction by no means healthy for the future of the medium.

CHAPTER 6

The Do-Gooders, Politicos, Pedagogues, and Assorted Other Ax Grinders

TELEVISION HAS ALWAYS HAD ITS CRITICS

Television, almost from its inception in the late '40s, has been under a steady barrage from concerned critics representing every corner of society. For almost 40 years now pro-social advocates have continued to circle television's wagon train, and while television keeps fending off all the attacks, still they come. Even Lee De Forest, inventor of the Audion tube, and later sound-on-film pictures and high speed transmission, questioned whether television was a blessing or a curse. He wondered if he had helped create a "benign Frankenstein." In the early '50s, important clerics and educators were already saying the world would have been a happier place without television and some prophesied that our society would eventually forget how to read and write. Literary critics, dramatists, and serious actors and actresses all chimed in to declare television a cultural calamity and barbarism of the worst sort. Poet and critic, John Ciardi, said children were watching shows hosted by "sickening oafs."

In the early '50s, one religious association sponsored a movement to disallow children to be alone in front of the television set. The Pilot Radio Corporation developed a television set equipped with heavy doors and a bronze lock.

Doctors joined in the growing criticism. One Wisconsin chiropodist warned that children could be stricken with bad feet as a result of inactivity. Another Cleveland specialist voiced concern about frog knees or *Frogi-*

tis caused by sitting in front of the television set with legs folded back. And still another doctor diagnosed a television-related affliction as *TV Bottom.* All sorts of complaints from children such as cramps, headaches, stomach spasms, and pains were blamed on watching television.

In time, the weight of scientific proof dispelled all the notions of TV Bottom, TV Tummy, and TV Squint, but the criticism of television's influence on children did not abate. The effects of television on children is an issue of major concern and the debates continue to rage and the researchers continue to churn out new findings. Today, in the fourth generation of television in the United States, the question of television's existence is no longer the issue. Today, the critical view is focused on a handful of subjects:

- gratuitous violence
- sexual and racial stereotyping
- the educational or uplifting content of children's shows
- commercials for children—primarily, their excessive number, and those concerned with nutrition, dental health, and expensive toys

CRITICIZING CHILDREN'S TELEVISION IS A POPULAR TOPIC

Most of the published literature about children's television has argued that television is harmful to children; yet, few of these critics have been able to prove their points conclusively. Any effort in the welfare of children in the United States is generally viewed as a pro-social act deserving admiration and respect. It doesn't matter if the criticism is ill-founded or the solutions recommended are impractical, the argument is well-meaning and therefore valid. In this regard, television for children has become a popular subject to beat on. It's fair game for everyone. Because most television for children appears to be mindless entertainment without substantive values, it invites criticism as obviously as a punching bag invites you to take a whack at it. Because it is so easy to obtain sympathy and agreement about the evils of children's television, the reformers of children's television have been able to create a small industry in itself and some politicians, over the past 40 years, have used the topic to gain favorable personal exposure and win votes.

IF YOU DON'T KNOW WHAT'S WRONG, YOU CAN'T FIX IT

This discourse on children's television is pragmatic and takes a business-man's point of view. The temptation to put up a defense for children's television does arise. Instead, I would merely like to highlight the prominent issues and some of the more notable reforms, indicating a few of the successes and failures. No one interested in children's television can grasp the subject without understanding what its aches and pains have been, what specific things its critics have found wrong with it, and what the reformers are trying to do with it other than abolish it entirely. There has been so much controversy that anyone with any interest in television is forced to cope with it. Equally important, the controversy has influenced the government's point of view about regulation and prompted federal agencies to consider changes that would seriously affect the marketplace.

THE PROTEST AGAINST TELEVISED VIOLENCE

One of the earliest public voices to speak against aggression on television was Senator Thomas Dodd of Connecticut. While Dodd was a Democrat, he was neither a liberal nor a conservative. Rather, he was an oldtime politician who knew how to turn issues into headlines. He built a career on this uncanny ability.

Dodd was followed by another powerful political figure, Senator John Pastore of Rhode Island, a former Chairman of the Senate Commerce Committee's influential Communication's Subcommittee. Senator Pastore began a well-organized assault on televised aggression in 1968, a battle that resulted in the Surgeon General's investigation over the next four years. The investigation ended with a report but no policy recommendation.

Senator Pastore was frustrated by the report's absence of a policy recommendation. The scientists who made an exhaustive study of the subject were unable to reach strong enough conclusions to translate into public policy. Yet Senator Pastore, who had become the symbolic leader for all of the pro-social critics attacking television, requested the Secretary of HEW and the FCC to publish an annual violence index to measure the amount of televised violence entering American homes.

The Surgeon General's report, which appeared in 1972, attempted to answer the question of whether the viewing of television violence stimulates aggressive behavior in young children. The research is reported in five volumes of articles spanning almost 2,500 pages. In these volumes, the authors of the research write in their own words. In a separate volume, the Surgeon General's Advisory Committee on Television and Social Behavior offers a cautious interpretation of the new studies as well as some consideration of earlier research on the topic. Because the evidence is inconclusive, a debate emerged—one that continues to this day. The Surgeon General's Advisory Committee, while acknowledging flaws in many of the individual studies, held that the convergence of evidence was sufficient to permit only a qualified conclusion about the causal relationship between the excessive viewing of violence and later aggressive behavior. This qualified conclusion was adopted by some researchers and rejected by others. In the face of these hazy and inconclusive results, Senator Pastore put the networks on notice that he and his senatorial colleagues would no longer tolerate television's "endless repetition of the message that conflict may be resolved by aggression."

In retrospect, both Senator Dodd's and Senator Pastore's activities in attacking televised violence are historically important because they became rallying points for a group of ladies in Boston, a handful of pedagogues, and professors of human development whose subsequent efforts were to make some tangible change in network policy during the years following the '60s—changes the Senators were unable to make.

While the HEW and the FCC did not publish an annual violence index as Pastore requested, George Gerbner, Dean of the Annenberg School of Communications at the University of Pennsylvania, took up the task of counting the violent incidents on television and compiled an astonishing list of statistics. Gerbner and some trained observers studied television from 1967 to 1972. They recorded the number of violent episodes on prime-time television and Saturday morning cartoons during one week in October as representative of each year's programming.

Given Gerbner's broad definition of violence and aggression—any antisocial behavior in goal seeking—the results of this research are not so startling. In 1969 for example, eight out of ten shows contained violence, with five violent episodes per show. Further, the most violent programs were cartoons designed for children. The average cartoon hour in 1967, according to Gerbner studies, contained more than three times as many violent episodes as the average adult dramatic hour. By 1969 there was a violent episode at least every two minutes in all Saturday morning programming. The average cartoon had nearly twelve times the violence rate of the average movie hour. Obviously, pratfalls and other forms of animated slapstick were considered violent.

Gerbner is not the only social scientist to analyze violent programming content. Action for Children's Television, an organization started by some women in Boston (whose efforts will be detailed elsewhere in this chapter) commissioned Dr. F. Earle Barcus of Boston University in 1975 to examine the amount of violence on television seen by children in non-network time, 3:00 P.M. to 6:00 P.M. Barcus did a ten station analysis. In his report he indicates that "more than six of ten stories contained some observable act of violence, and about three in ten were 'saturated' with violent acts. Cartoon comedy and older action-adventure programs account for most of the violent episodes."

THE NETWORKS' EFFORTS TO CLEAN UP CARTOONS

Despite the fact that the Surgeon General's study showed no conclusive evidence of a correlation between televised violence and aggressive behavior in children, the report itself and the tallies of mayhem by Gerbner, Barcus, and others have exerted considerable influence on network programmers. In the spirit of self-regulation, the three networks initiated some pro-social standards to eliminate aggression from their Saturday morning cartoons.

Gary Grossman, author of a history entitled *Saturday Morning TV* states "Today, networks red-pencil any prolonged action that would so much as make a palm sweat." The networks' program practices departments, which literally operate as censors, rigorously enforce a pro-social policy that eliminates any "imitable behavior" which might be considered dangerous. One network cut out a scene showing a pussycat character in "Josie and the Pussycats" hiding from a monster in a dish of spaghetti. The cut was made on the grounds that some child might dunk his cat into pasta as well. "I can't even have a character throw a pie in someone's face anymore," says Joe Barbera of Hanna-Barbera, one of the networks' major suppliers of cartoon shows. "The reason is simple. It's imitable, and the networks say we can't do anything bad that a child might imitate."

Norm Prescott, formerly of Filmation, another major supplier of cartoons for the networks, says "The program practices departments outlined four major don'ts. No physical violence, no guns, no jeopardy, and no threats." Bill Scott, another major animator, notes, "Hyperbole is also out, which seems strange to me because animation in itself is a hyperbolic medium."

Each network now has a bible or a book of rules to which they adhere. Ordinarily the rules have a logic and a purpose, but it is easy to see how such restrictions do not make sense to the creators of programming. ABC has ruled that if a building is damaged or destroyed during a story, it must be completely repaired by the cartoon's finale. Gary Grossman also reported that on one occasion a production studio wanted to insert a message critical of dictators at the end of a cartoon. ABC reportedly allowed mention of Caesar and Napoleon, but not of Adolf Hitler since he was associated with fanaticism and violence.

One might well ask why did the networks overreact, and how did things get so out of hand? The only answer is that the networks have, over time, grown truly concerned about the effects of televised violence on children, and have become overprotective in their censorship for fear of possible government intervention. As in all things, when a situation is troubled and perceived as being sorely in need of reform, the pendulum swings too far.

Animation is a medium that depends on speed, action, and very broad slapstick humor. Good must defeat evil in a highly visible way, often leading to exaggerated pratfalls or wild forms of sandbagging. Villains must be clearly punished, but in crazy and humorous ways. The networks have now eliminated all that. In today's network cartoons, the wicked are merely foiled. The scene quickly changes and they are left scot-free, presumably because punishment would be too violent.

Without suggesting that we turn once again to violent solutions to the inevitable good versus evil stories, it should be shown that in many ways the new pro-social campaign to rid cartoons of aggression and violence also betrays the real interests of children. The new network cartoon is so sanitized it deprives children of the very promise of justice itself. Curiously enough, you can now point to the fairy tales, which every child learns in books, as being far more filled with stories of violent justice than what they are watching today on Saturday morning network television. How else would you end the story of "The Three Little Pigs" if the Big Bad Wolf didn't fall into the pot of boiling water?

STEREOTYPES AND ROLE MODELS

For children who spend three or four hours a day watching television, the television world becomes their world. Society portrayed on television is often distorted when held up to reality. This concept is especially true for children entrenched in homogenous white communities who are not familiar with blacks, Hispanics, or a broader cross section of society. In that respect, and in television's portrayal of women, the elderly, the handi-capped, and certain occupational workers, television has been harshly criticized. These distortions have caused concern among parents, educators, and special interest groups who believe the potential effect of these inaccuracies is considerable.

It is natural to expect television to reflect society's sex ratio—50 percent male and 50 percent female. According to George Gerbner's count, however, between 66 and 75 percent of all television roles in the first 25 years of its history were male. In addition, though women now constitute about half of the nation's labor force, only about 20 percent of the television roles having a specific occupational activity are held by women.

In an article entitled "From Olive Oyl to Sweet Polly Purebred: Sex Role Stereotype and Televised Cartoons" by R. M. Levinson, this investigator found that females on Saturday morning cartoons have a far more restricted range of occupational roles than males. Females in cartoon kids' shows usually appear as pretty females in adolescence and housewives in adulthood. Their status is defined by their relationship to males. Females are shown as less likely to accomplish tasks.

In addition, it is clear to even the most casual observer that men and women from diverse racial and ethnic groups are presented in very restricted and biased ways on television. The formal social-occupational status of blacks and Hispanics has been considerably improved since the early days of television when blacks were cast as lovable buffoons ("Amos and Andy") or servants. Today, both groups are usually shown as responsible citizens, but they are still vastly underrepresented.

Two other large minority groups, the aged and the handicapped, have also been neglected on television. More than 30 million people in the United States are over 60 years old, yet television has virtually ignored them as a major segment of the population. Television seldom provides successful models for aging. When handicapped or disabled people are shown on television, the plot is usually about a tragic individual who wants to overcome obstacles to lead a meaningful life. They are seldom treated in normal life situations, in normal settings, equal to their peers; rather, they become objects of pity.

Obviously, television has a difficult job trying to portray all groups fairly. The ideal situation would be for television to portray the widest possible range of people to reflect our society as it is in the real world, yet, writers of drama or comedy do not start a script by a nose count of sexes, races, or ages. Even the most well-intentioned writers find it difficult to satisfy every group all of the time. Someone is always left out or possibly included and then misinterpreted. The one whose ox is gored is the one with the most vocal complaint.

My personal experience as a creator of television programming for children has shown me just how difficult it is to be entirely fair and realistic. In 1980, a few months after the start of Nickelodeon, the cable network for children, I accepted the challenge of managing and pioneering the fledgling network. Almost from the first day I initiated a policy for Nickelodeon not unlike that of the BBC. Nickelodeon would air no entertainment that was not uplifting, inspiring, informative, or educational. We would not show violence as entertainment, and would shy away from stereotyping of any kind—sexual, racial, or by age. During my three and a half years at Nickelodeon, we rigidly adhered to that policy for 14 televised hours per day. Our record, compared to commercial television, was spotless. But we still received complaints.

In an effort to show children some heroes and heroines (and a few villains) of the real world, I created an award-winning show entitled "Against the Odds." The show consisted of 26 half-hours of biographies of famous men and women in history, people who achieved great fame against considerable odds. Each half-hour consisted of two contrasting or comparable stories that were somehow related. The first episode was about Winston Churchill and Joan of Arc. Both were political warriors called upon by their people to defend their countries—one in the nuclear age, and the other in the age of bows and arrows. The shows, produced in Los Angeles by Klein &, were created out of stock footage, still photos, paintings, sculpture, and any other graphic material available, welded together to tell a relatively simple and juvenilized version of famous peoples' lives and exploits.

In another half-hour, we contrasted two Italian immigrants of the 1920s who skyrocketed to international fame for a very short few years, and then died prematurely. Each chose a different path. The two men were Rudolph Valentino and Al Capone—one a hero of sorts, the other a gangster. Based on the show's publicity alone, we received reprimanding letters from Italian-American organizations. Copies of the letters were sent to every Italian-American politician in New York including Governor Cuomo. The objections were that we dared to choose Al Capone as a subject.

The same problem came up when we did a show comparing and contrasting Napoleon and Adolf Hitler as military dictators who had conquered Europe. The Anti-Defamation League of the B'Nai Brith was upset because we were showing an episode about Hitler to children, despite the fact that he was characterized as a fanatic and a villain.

Bill Bixby hosted "Against the Odds," a series on Nickelodeon that explores the personalities and careers of famous heroes and heroines whose achievements helped mold history. (Courtesy, Nickelodeon)

Evidently my explanatory responses to those organizations were calming because I was subsequently invited to appear on a symposium with other broadcasters to discuss television's treatment of ethnic groups. It turned out to be a genuine learning experience. I felt it was quite natural for Italian-Americans to be heatedly vocal in their objections to television's treatment of Italians as mafiosos or waiters. But when they jumped on the Lt. Frank Furillo character in "Hill Street Blues," I was truly astonished. It seems that some Italian-Americans feel that Lt. Frank Furillo is not a good Italian-American role model because he was interested in another woman while not yet divorced, he did not visit his son often enough, and he hardly ever phoned his parents. The prevailing opinion was that no self-respecting Italian man would behave in such a manner.

It was then, for the first time, I realized that no matter how hard the creators of television try to cope with issues of stereotyping, it is impossible to be entirely successful. Criticism and complaints are inevitable.

THE NETWORKS' EFFORTS TO MAKE QUALITY PROGRAMMING

While FCC Commissioner Newton Minow was not the first to excoriate the broadcast industry, or to point out the lack of quality programming for children, in 1961 his voice was the loudest and clearest. His landmark "vast wasteland" speech condemning networks and stations for poor quality shows, along with his threat to remove licenses, resounded throughout the broadcast industry. Minow described children's programs in 1961 as "dull, gray, and insipid as dishwater, just as tasteless, just as nourishing." He called upon creative television professionals to produce shows that would enrich the minds and spirits of children. Minow implored each network to devote at least two afternoons per week to good, educational programming for children.

NBC responded with "One, Two, Three-Go" and "Exploring." CBS introduced "Reading Room" and ABC launched "Discovery," an afternoon weekday series. All of these shows were well-intentioned, educational efforts, but for the most part, programmed amidst the Saturday morning cartoons. Despite the fact they didn't get much of an audience, the shows were sponsored by more enlightened advertisers—at first. The advertisers eventually lost heart and were not willing to pay high rates for poorly rated shows. They preferred to concentrate their money on the cartoon shows where the audience was.

THE FUNNY COMPANY: AN EARLY ATTEMPT AT EDUTAINMENT

The poor ratings for the new network educational shows made it apparent that children would not watch instructive, schoolroom type material unless it was encapsulated in a more entertaining format. In an article in *Broadcasting Magazine* dated December 24, 1962, I outlined this problem and suggested the solution lay in something called "edutainment." At the time, I didn't know exactly what that was, but indicated I would search for an idea along those lines and get it on the air. I knew that Mattel would support it if we could find the right format.

A few months later a producer named Ken Snyder showed us, in script and storyboard form, what we had been looking for. It was a new kind of cartoon show called "The Funny Company."

"The Funny Company" was about an enterprising club of neighborhood children and their friends (including a big bird named Terry Dactyl) who used their collective wits and energy to a wholesome purpose. The kids, not unlike a junior achievement club, made money at odd jobs—cleaning out attics, printing hand bills, and selling items and services. The kids had a clubhouse, of course, and within it was a sort of computer or information machine invented by a boy genius named Jasper N. Park with some help from a friendly, elderly neighbor. The machine, called the Wisenheimer, enabled the kids to get necessary information to get the club's work done.

The Weisenheimer was also used as a story device to cleverly sandwich two-minute educational elements between the regular cartoon segments. Each episode was designed like a sugarcoated pill, with educational centers about natural and physical science, other lands and peoples, business and industry, sports, hobbies, folklore, and how-to subjects.

With Mattel's financial backing and under the agency's direction, Snyder produced the show in an unusual format. There were 260 individual five-minute episodes. Recognizing that stations across the country were looking for something like "edutainment" in response to Minow's speech, my associate Eddie Smardan devised a brilliant plan to barter the series to stations in exchange for time. "The Funny Company" was launched on September 9, 1963, and over the next three years we were able to play in 117 markets. It was an innovation not only in quality programming, but in the novel barter arrangement itself. Stations played "The Funny Company" as five-minute episodes, quarter-hours, and complete half-hours. Most importantly, it was a way to make quality programming acceptable to kids and worthwhile for an advertiser to support.

THE NETWORKS KEEP TRYING

When the first attempts at airing better programming failed financially, the networks lost heart and when the pressure from government sources abated, they went back to business as usual. Instead of trying to improve the usual cartoon fare and expand Saturday morning schedules with more creative programming, they filled the time slots of Saturday morning with reruns of "Make Room for Daddy," "Roy Rogers," "Rin-Tin-Tin," and "My Friend Flicka."

It wasn't until the late '60s that the networks, feeling some oncoming pressure from the FCC once again, started filling open commercial time with educational and inspirational inserts considered pro-social. CBS started "In the News" in 1970 and ABC started "After School Specials," dramas for older kids, 10-14, aimed at helping kids better understand themselves. CBS also launched a variety of children's special programs based on the lively arts. None of these efforts interfered with the usual Saturday morning cartoon fare, but they were concrete evidence to critics that the networks did care sufficiently about more highbrow programming for children, and were willing to invest time and money in that programming despite the fact there was no possibility whatsoever of earning profits from these shows.

During this period, one network executive consistently produced highly regarded programming, George Heineman at NBC. In the early years he created "Ding Dong School" and "Hi Mom" at WRCA. Then at NBC he was the first network vice-president appointed for children's programs, and while there, he created "Take a Giant Step" and "Go," both informative, uplifting shows for kids. In 1971, Heineman was given a special Peabody award for the individual shows he had done and his work on the "NBC Children's Theater."

"Mr. Rogers" and "Sesame Street"

What we now know as public television started as a loosely knit group of educational stations back in the '50s. Unencumbered by the need to get ratings and advertising revenues, the goals of these stations were solely to inform and educate. But their first productions were so dull and boring they attracted few children. No child would watch a math or a science lesson when he or she could easily flip the dial to something more entertaining.

When these stations were amalgamated into a Public Television Network in 1967, one of television's longest running and finest children's shows was also launched, "Mr. Roger's Neighborhood." Fred Rogers' soft approach for preschoolers has since made him into one of television's most beloved hosts. He continues to this day, still working at his lifelong goal of creating "an atmosphere where children are accepted and allowed to grow."

Two years after "Mr. Rogers" was launched, children's television took a spectacular leap in quality with the advent of "Sesame Street." This show was really the first to combine the fast pace of commercial television with an actual educational lesson plan.

The "Sesame Street" series, which has become an institution with lasting significance, was originally funded by the Carnegie, Ford, and Markle Foundations and the U.S. Office of Education. The first season's shows cost more than $8 million.

"*Sesame Street,*" with its many famous Muppet characters, offers proof that entertainment and education can be combined into programming that will attract preschool children and hold them. (Courtesy, Children's Television Workshop)

"Sesame Street's" chief visionary was Joan Ganz Cooney, head of the Children's Television Workshop. She was able to raise the funds for this new experiment because of the show's original goals of teaching letter and number skills to disadvantaged ghetto children. Each show featured a different letter or number and contained quick, staccato messages similar to the catchy phrases or jingles in television commercials. Curiously enough, Ken Snyder, the producer we had worked with earlier to create "The Funny Company," designed the prototypes and produced the first 200 of the animated learning segments.

The show was originally designed as a weekday, hour-long show that would play once a day. The public television network, however, had little else to air and most stations played it twice a day, and even more. In some markets "Sesame Street" was seen 17 or 18 times a week. For the first few years, the viewing audience of individual episodes was small. But without competition or the need to impress advertisers with ratings, the show just continued to be there all of the time. Eventually, it became a favorite show for preschoolers and parents alike, and its weekly cumulative audience grew to more than nine million homes.

George Woolery, in his book *Children's Television: The First Thirty-Five Years, 1946-1981,* points out "the series has been charged by critics as an expensive, overstimulating, irrelevant, and misguided educational vehicle that has failed in its most important task, that of narrowing the gap between advantaged and disadvantaged children." Psychologists Jerome and Dorothy Singer have also argued that "Sesame Street," with a formula paced so fast "that as soon as a child starts to understand one sequence, he must digest another completely different sequence," has helped to create a generation of speed freaks.

I find it interesting that even the best intentioned children's television, the first truly successful format to combine entertainment and education, a show that has lasted almost 20 years *without* advertising, still has critics who find it wanting. There are reformers who want to reform the reformers, and do-gooders who want to outdo the do-gooders.

Part of the reason for "Sesame Street's" great international success (it now plays in more than 50 countries) is the Muppet characters originally created by Jim Henson. Generations of preschoolers have found delight in Kermit the Frog (Henson's voice), a seven foot tall yellow canary named Big Bird, Oscar the Grouch, Cookie Monster, Bert and Ernie, Grover, and all the rest. The clever use of these characters interacting with the children and guests of "Sesame Street" has made them quickly identifiable favorites, and a licensing gold mine for the Children's Television Workshop.

Joan Ganz Cooney was once quoted as saying, "If we as a total society put the interest of our children first, then we are led to the inescapable conclusion that it is terribly wrong to be pitching products at the young. It is like shooting fish in a barrel. It is grotesquely unfair." Strange words from the president of a company that now licenses more than 1,700 items for children under the "Sesame Street" name that sell about $200 million a year at wholesale. CTW's revenues from those products are more than $40 million a year. Ms. Cooney points out that these funds are needed to produce new episodes of "Sesame Street," which now cost more than $9 million a year. Public broadcasting provides only five percent of CTW's budget and federal funding has been erratic. In addition, CTW's two other shows for older children "The Electric Company" and "3-2-1 Contact," relied on government and private underwriting and have now come to an end.

Following the reports on CTW in such financial publications as *Forbes Magazine* and the business pages of the *New York Times,* one concludes that the people at CTW sound like adolescents—they talk about ethics and keep asking for money. They do not understand why federal funding is so niggardly and why corporate donors, which they call underwriters, are so difficult to come by. One of the reasons, perhaps, is that the government, and major corporations that strongly believe in free enterprise, are growing increasingly cautious about so-called non-profit companies who ask for funding. One chairman of a major packaged goods company told me, "We gave 'Sesame Street' a substantial contribution for a while and it gave us a nice warm feeling, but that's about all we got out of it. That, and a slide on television indicating we had provided some funding. That isn't enough to justify that kind of expenditure to our stockholders. Besides," he went on, "when the television we supported helped them develop popular characters they could license, I didn't see them offering to share any of the royalties with us."

Despite the criticism aimed at it, there is no question that "Sesame Street" was and is an important television development for younger children. Artistically, it offers proof that entertainment and education *can* be combined into programming that will attract preschool children and hold them. However, for do-gooders to point to "Sesame Street" as a prime example of how all commercial television should be is to lose sight of CTW's unique position as a production company. First of all, they are tax-exempt because of the educational nature of their products. Second, what other company has had the advantage of over $100 million in funding without any obligation whatsoever to repay its debt?

Now that CTW is facing hungry times because funding is evaporating, they are turning towards the creation of programming in a rare commercial format. *Forbes Magazine* states that their "holier than thou attitudes have shifted with time and necessity," and pointed out that CTW's "decision to become more clearly commercial is made easier by changing demographics. As members of the so-called baby-boom generation have learned to stop worrying and love moneymaking, so are they willing to let Children's Television Workshop do the same. That means cash for CTW. Big Bird is growing up. Maybe next he'll become a taxpayer".

PEGGY CHARREN, "ACT'S GRINDER"

Peggy Charren has the remarkable ability to point out some unfortunate ironies, some lamentable contradictions, and on more than one occasion some sad but inevitable truths.

As an organizer and spokeswoman for reform, she has accomplished more to change children's television than any other person. Despite the fact that she has lost considerably more battles than she's won, and the changes she has been able to effect are relatively insignificant in the larger scheme of things, she has certainly heightened the consciousness of broadcasters, producers, and advertisers everywhere. For that reason alone, her efforts as the leader of the most notable and vocal consumerist group in children's television commands our special attention.

Peggy Charren is the founder and president of Action for Children's Television (ACT), a non-profit, public interest group whose main purpose has been to demand change in children's television. The group started in Peggy Charren's living room in Newtonville, a suburb of Boston, in 1968. It has since grown to national proportions with a volunteer membership between 15,000 and 20,000. It also has a yearly budget reported to fall between $300,000 and $400,000. These funds come from public, private, and federal sources. The yearly budget goes for salaries for an attorney, an assistant director, publicity coordinator, and other employees. It also pays for office rent, publication costs, consultants, legal fees, transportation, and correspondence. For the relatively little money ACT has had to work with, they have made a very big noise.

Initially, ACT had the express goal of eliminating commercials from children's viewing hours. In 1970, ACT filed a petition along those lines with the FCC. It subsequently filed a petition with the FTC to prohibit selling of toys to children on television, and followed that petition with another to prohibit the selling of edibles to children on television. They then filed complaints against three major drug companies for advertising vitamins to children.

As a result of these petitions, government agencies held hearings and studied all the questions raised but did not rule on any of them. The three major drug companies agreed to end vitamin advertising on children's commercial television. They did so as a result of ACT's petition, *before* the FTC took any action whatsoever.

Because of ACT pressure, in 1973 the National Association of Broadcasters indicated new code rules stating 1) A host of a television show for children could not appear in commercials, and 2) Commercials on network children's shows would be cut to 12 minutes per hour. Two years later, under continued pressure from ACT, the National Code Board cut the amount of commercial time from 12 to 10 minutes per hour and to nine and a half minutes on weekends. While the end result of these reductions has been to eliminate clutter, it has also raised advertising costs, but in many ways has made the advertising more effective. The higher prices have eliminated the small advertiser and reduced competition. The airing of fewer commercials improves retention of individual ones.

In 1973, ACT filed specific complaints with the FTC against cereal and candy companies and later complained about specific commercials from candy and toy companies that used deceptive advertising.

For a brief while in ACT's crusade, they seemed to have the ear of the FCC. In 1980, the group petitioned the FCC with a proposal that would require each television station to broadcast a minimum amount of children's programming each day. This was near the end of the Carter administration, and for a time, it looked as if the FCC might act on the proposal. Charles Ferris, the FCC chairman at the time, was a supporter of some type of minimum requirement.

With the Reagan administration, ACT's children's programming proposals have gone virtually unheeded. Mark Fowler, the new chairman of the FCC, has not been sympathetic to ACT's concerns. Fowler's philosophy has been to leave broadcasting up to the broadcasters and "let the marketplace decide."

Peggy Charren's charge is that the marketplace allows broadcasters to broadcast only shows that get high ratings and make big money. That point of view, she contends, automatically eliminates programming with any quality and the kids end up with an empty plate. There is a certain amount of truth in this lament because it is a comment on the way our broadcast system works. But what ACT considers quality programming for children is considered soft and unexciting by the broadcast industry and there is only so much of it they will support.

Peggy Charren and ACT continue to flail away in Washington with efforts to improve the quality of children's programming. In recent years she has enlisted the aid of House Representative Timothy Wirth (D-Colorado) to pass a bill that would impose a quota on broadcasters. FCC Commissioner Henry Rivera also joined her camp and became, for a while, highly vocal on the subject of children's television. The bill has not yet been passed.

Most recently Peggy Charren and ACT have taken up protesting the so-called half-hour commercials, the new television series based on a line of toy products. ACT has once again petitioned the FCC on this matter. New rulings are not likely to be established. Mark Fowler, Chairman of the FCC, pointed out that the entire broadcast spectrum, including public television and cable, has more children's programming than ever before and because much of it on cable is high quality, there is no need to regulate it or impose quotas. With almost revolutionary fervor, Peggy Charren has seriously criticized Fowler's "let them eat cable" attitude.

It is abundantly clear, after ACT's 16 years of campaigning for improved children's television, that the real villain in ACT's act is the advertiser. On one hand, Ms. Charren continually points out that most advertisers are not interested in reaching children. To demonstrate her point that children have no voice in controlling what television offers them she says, "children don't have any money. They don't have power and the only advertisers that want to reach them are the sugary food and expensive toy manufacturers." On the other hand she is quick to point out that hundreds of millions of dollars are spent every year in advertising to exploit children on television. The fact that there would be virtually no children's television without the advertising support seems to be of little consequence. Since no other solutions have been forthcoming, ACT obviously expects children's television to be funded by the government, by broadcasters themselves, or by the stockholders of major corporations.

Despite a good deal of this kind of fuzzy thinking and a lack of concern for pragmatic realities, ACT has done a remarkable job of putting advertisers, broadcasters, and the government on the hot seat. Once dismissed as being part of the lunatic fringe, ACT is now taken seriously by the broadcast and children's advertising industry.

Because she is always willing to comment freely without corporate restraint on behalf of ACT's causes, the press has made Peggy Charren into a media guru of sorts. She has become the standard bearer for the improvement of children's television. Articles on children's television in the press seldom fail to include some quote or statement from Peggy Charren. ACT's National Symposiums on children and television are well attended. Despite the fact that there are few specific criteria for the ACT Achievement

Awards in Children's television and the people judging the entries are not particularly qualified, major producers submit their programs in this award competition and show up at the award ceremonies. The networks and other broadcasters, bamboozled by ACT, have invested millions of dollars both trying to win ACT's approval and defending themselves at hearings in Washington.

One must question whether these reactions on the part of industry are done out of genuine respect for ACT's efforts or to curry favor with Peggy Charren. No one wants ACT stirring up their pot. But, it appears to me, after all these years, Peggy Charren and ACT's power is more a creation of the press than a reality. I had an opportunity to test the efficacy of this citizens' group in 1983 when I was managing Nickelodeon, the children's cable network.

When Nickelodeon was started in late 1979 it was conceived as a service funded by cable operators. To carry the 14-hour per day service on their system, cable operators paid the Warner-Amex Satellite Entertainment Company, the parent of Nickelodeon, ten cents per subscription per month. As the network became more popular and more expensive to operate, the rate was hiked to 15 cents. Because it was providing high quality original programming, the network was still running at a loss and another rate increase was contemplated. When we tested the water on a rate increase with our cable operator customers we discovered they would not stand still for another cent. Many threatened to cancel the service. The only solution to our economic survival was to take advertising. We had already experimented unsuccessfully with a form of underwriting similar to that used in public television.

When we announced our intentions (and our reasons) to begin accepting advertising on Nickelodeon, the squawks from ACT in the trade press were loud and clear. ACT immediately sent out a special mailer to all its members urging them to petition Nickelodeon not to take advertising.

When we saw the mailer we girded ourselves for a deluge of mail. I asked our mail service people to direct all such mail to my office. I was prepared to answer each protester personally, even if I had to write several thousand letters.

Over the next few months, much to our surprise, we did not receive a single petition. Beyond six postal cards and the same number of letters, we didn't hear a thing—not from ACT members and not from subscribers to the channel. And certainly not from the children who regularly sent us thousands of letters about all manners of things. While the issue of advertising to children may be at the heart of ACT's charter and purpose, based on this experience, at least, it is certainly not a burning consumer issue.

Only a dozen protest letters from over 21 million subscribers has to tell you something.

THE MARKETPLACE CONTINUES TO DECIDE

The fact that television, particularly children's television, is a sitting duck inviting pot shots from every quarter has historically made it an easy target for criticism. Television's obvious failings over the past 40 years have created an environment in which the do-gooders, the politicos, the pedagogues, and various other ax grinders have thrived. Criticizing television is as American as motherhood and apple pie. Any act to improve it gains immediate sympathy.

While reformers have been distrustful of marketplace thinking, it is all to the broadcast industry's credit that significant changes have gradually occurred without the government intervention some advocates have demanded. Some examples follow:

- Violence in children's television has been curbed.
- There is a heightened sensitivity to stereotyping.
- There is less advertising clutter.
- There is more enlightening programming for children than ever before.

These improvements occurred without burdening broadcasters with useless government rules and stifling restrictions on business practices. Perhaps they would not have come about without the hue and cry from the would-be reformers, but the marketplace has made steady progress. Because the government agencies have been consistently reluctant to interfere with business, the reformers have discovered, in the '80s, that improving children's television is a lot like eating an artichoke, you must go through a lot to get very little. The difficulties of legislation may not be worth it. A more powerful force is the broadcast industry's genuine interest in the public as well as in profits. Its efforts at self-regulation are slowly proving effective.

In a recent speech to the National Association of Broadcasters, FCC Chairman Mark Fowler praised the marketplace approach he has endorsed for five years and said that by giving broadcasters more freedom and choice it has "forced people in government to realize what everybody else does—that the broadcasting business is a business."

CHAPTER 7

Entering the Boom Years

THE '80S HAVE USHERED IN BOOM YEARS FOR CHILDREN'S TELEVISION. NEVER before in the history of the medium has there been such an abundance of children's television of every kind. It is now difficult to imagine that only a few years ago those of us involved in the children's television business were seriously worried whether children's television would survive at all.

Looking back on it today one must wonder what all the tumult and shouting was about in the '70s and whether it was totally out of proportion with the problems that then existed. Did all the carping and the threats of government intervention reflect a true public opinion? What did the television audience really think about television, particularly children's television, 10 and 20 years ago and what do they think about it today? What brought about the sudden and explosive growth of children's television in this decade?

THE CONCERNS ABOUT SURVIVAL IN THE '70S

In the early '70s, every advertising agency that represented a major children's advertiser was asked a pressing question: What alternatives do we have in the event the curtain rings down on advertising on children's television? In my own experience I was asked to prepare a white paper on this subject at least a half dozen times. The answers were, for the most part, always the same. If children's advertising is abolished on commercial television, there is no other way to reach the 2 to 12 year old audience as efficiently.

There was radio, but it no longer played children's material. The Sunday newspaper comics have always been more of an adult medium. That left comic books and children's magazines for the over six-year olds who can read. Comic books have a large circulation and readership, but these publications have long lead times and poor reproduction. In addition they are not always acceptable in the home and are consequently a poor environment for advertising believability. Other children's magazines have, in comparison with television, an insignificant circulation.

Today, one would also have to point to cable television and VCRs as budding mediums, cable already being reasonably developed in almost half the nation. The conclusions, however, would be the same. Children's commercial television has become the life blood of many large businesses and it is hard to imagine many cereal companies, toy companies, candy, cookie, and non-carbonated drink companies functioning well without it. The investments in these products are too great, and too important to industry and broadcasting, to allow any consumerist movement or government agency to legislate them out of business.

The consumerist movement tried to persuade the government to take regulatory steps in the past, but more or less peaked before the Reagan Administration and has made no significant inroads since. In a different administration it is conceivable there could be some renewed action to ban children's advertising on television. It is obvious that ACT and other consumerist groups are still struggling to achieve that end. So it is still possible, but just barely. To convince the government to intervene would require a lot of legislation and more boat-rocking than either political party wants to risk. Beyond that, there is so much at stake because the children's products business has grown so large that any attempts at regulation affecting advertising would be fought fiercely for years in the courts.

WILL THE CONSUMERIST MOVEMENT CONTINUE?

Children's television has been a beleaguered industry for more than 30 years. It has been scorned by the intelligentsia, condemned by moralists and academicians, and ridiculed by the press. Still it has flourished. It flourished even during the height of consumerist demands in the '70s.

As long as children are thought to be defenseless in the face of television, the problem of advertising to children will continue to be a controversial issue. Many of our educators are contemptuous of commerce, of buying and selling, and are naive about human behavior in the marketplace. Children's advertising, for this group, is commercial vulgarity in its purest form.

Politicians are always looking for issues that will bring them support at the ballot box. The best are always motherhood issues. Very few issues create fewer active opponents than the regulation of advertising to children. When so little has been accomplished in terms of government regulation, it is difficult to understand why the reformers and consumer advocates continue their struggle. After closely watching these activists for more than 30 years, I must conclude it seems typical of regulatory zeal not to care whether activism achieves its objective. Militating for reform appears to be an end in itself. These activists, intellectuals for the most part, are a funny breed. They value freedom of speech and freedom of thought for themselves, but advocate control and censorship for everybody else.

Apparently it makes no difference that the consumerists do not represent the consumer at large. The public is certainly not clamoring for changes in television or creating regulatory pressure. Complaints from people who complain about television commercials addressed to children account for less than two percent of the advertising complaints the National Advertising Review Board receives. While there is evidence that the nation's viewing audience has grown somewhat more disenchanted with television over the past 30 years, America's love affair with television continues and very little audience has been lost.

It is difficult to predict whether or not the heightened activity of the consumerist '70s will ever return. One thing is certain—consumer agitation is not popular this decade. The FTC is less active and there are more pressing problems than toys, cereals, and candy bars. The complaints regarding marketing and advertising to children are much fewer and there is very little public discussion of what's being sold to children and how.

Consumerists who once wanted to ban all advertising to children have surely taken note of recent events in French-speaking Canada. In 1980 the television authorities in Quebec banned all advertising to children under 13. In September 1986, that law was ruled in violation of Canada's Charter of Rights and Freedoms. The only result of the ban was that French-Canadian children started turning to U.S. cable broadcasting. The real effect of the law was that broadcasters no longer had any incentive to produce new programs.

There will undoubtedly be new consumer issues in the future. The only thing predictable about regulatory zeal is that it occurs in mature states during the best of times when there is peace and plenty. To make problems that do exist meaningful, they have to be blown all out of proportion and wildly exaggerated. That has happened with children's television off and on for the past 30 years. What form regulatory zeal's next moulting will take is difficult to say, but if past is prologue, any reactive changes brought about by dissent will be relatively insignificant.

TODAY'S PUBLIC OPINION ABOUT TELEVISION AND CHILDREN

It is fair to say that what people think about television—good or ill—has little to do with how much they watch. There are more television sets and television households today than ever before and the average hours of household television usage have climbed from five and a half hours per day in 1955 to more than seven hours today. The increase over the past 30 years has been steady.

Despite all the criticism leveled at Saturday morning children's television between 8:00 A.M. and 1:00 P.M., viewership of the three networks has fallen off only slightly—from 79 percent of households with children under 12 in 1975 to 77 percent of the same households in 1985. (Incidentally, "Bugs Bunny" and Hanna-Barbera's "Scooby Doo" were among the top Saturday morning shows in 1975, and were still among the top shows in 1985. The types of shows haven't changed that much.)

When extensive surveys are taken asking people what they like and dislike about television and what they think about its influence on children, the public's evaluation of television shows a decline since 1960. Three massive surveys have been made: Gary Steiner's "The People Look at Television" in 1963, Robert T. Bower's "Television and the Public" in 1973, and Robert T. Bower's "The Changing Television Audience in America" in 1985. In 1960, 30 percent of the population thought children would be better off without television; in 1970, only 24 percent agreed with this position, but in 1980, that negative view rose substantially to 36 percent. The principal objections to television have remained stable over the last 20 years with about half the survey feeling that children should not see violence, crime, sex, suggestiveness, or vulgarity. About a third of the sample cited activities children might do but don't because they're watching television, and there appears to be growing concern that television is a harmful interference to reading and schoolwork.

©1984 Hanna-Barbera Productions, Inc.

"Scooby Doo" has been one of the top Saturday morning shows for ten years. Scooby Doo is one of the newer characters to become a classic. (By permission of Hanna-Barbera Productions, Inc.)

Despite the fact that people are simply not as enthusiastic about television as they were 20 years ago, television on the whole still occupies a very positive place in the American mind. The majority of people are generally more favorable than not. Whatever decline television has experienced has been attributed to the changing television audience, which today is better educated. Education is a strong predictor of critical attitudes toward television.

It seems fair and realistic to assume that today's better educated parents do not look back at their childhood television viewing experience of 20 and 30 years ago as a negative one. They not only continue to be devoted to television themselves but are reluctant to monitor the amount of television their children are watching today. Obviously, there would not be so much children's television today if parents were encouraging their children to watch less of it. The increased number of children's programming hours are there because they are getting a substantial audience. If they weren't watching, the broadcasters would be playing something else.

THE WIDENING SPECTRUM OF CHILDREN'S TELEVISION

Until recent years children could watch television programming designed exclusively for them in only three forms: 1) network programming primarily on Saturday mornings, 2) local programming primarily on weekdays in daytime hours, and 3) public (and non-commercial) television all through the week in daytime hours. Of course, there has always been prime-time television after 8:00 P.M., but that programming, while heavily watched by children, is not created exclusively for them. Contrast that with what is available for children today: more weekday local programming than ever before, cable television in more than 45 percent of the country, and a vast library of children's programs on video cassettes. In addition there are more animated feature motion pictures at the theatres than ever before. Most of these films have been generated by the popularity of the same material on television.

For buyers of children's television advertising there are more opportunities today than they had in the history of the medium. At one time a children's television advertiser had only two choices: network or spot. Today, they can still buy network, but spot television has expanded so dramatically with syndicated children's shows that an advertiser can buy individual markets or virtually create a fourth network with a syndicated buy in a long market list covering most of the nation; a third force has emerged with cable television.

The result of all these new opportunities is that competition for children's advertising dollars has grown fierce. The combined billings for the three networks in children's Saturday morning advertising today is approximately $250 million or about three percent of the networks' total billings of an estimated $8.3 billion. Networks have been forced to drop their prices. At this time, the average price for a 30-second commercial for Saturday mornings in the fourth quarter of 1986 is about $24,800. During the fall quarter of 1985 the same 30-second commercial was averaging $26,700. Despite the drop in prices the networks have not been able to stem the flow of more and more dollars into syndication. At the end of the second quarter of 1986, several of the higher-rated syndication shows were already in sell-out positions.

Part of the reason for this shift in buying patterns is that advertising agencies and their clients are finding a more efficient cost per thousand price with higher-rated syndication shows. A syndicated buy in 80 percent of the country's markets may cost as little as $11,200 per 30-second commercial. Another reason, that particularly affects toy advertisers, is that the rules of the individual stations' program practices departments are not nearly so stringent regarding children's commercials as they are at the networks. This fact is causing the networks to reexamine and change some of their standards.

For example, in the June 9, 1986 issue of *Television/Radio Age,* it was reported that the networks required a commercial for Kenner's Care Bears to show each bear in the product line separately at the end of the commercial, accompanied by the bear's name. The result was that the advertiser wound up losing about nine seconds of commercial time in a 30-second commercial. For syndication, the requirements were only to mention the line of bears. This was certainly an influential factor affecting where the advertiser put his money.

THE EXPLOSIVE GROWTH OF SYNDICATION

A few years ago the production of animated children's shows was a tiny business confined to Saturday morning and syndicated reruns of successful Saturday shows during kids time on local television stations. A handful of producers dominated the business: Hanna-Barbera, Filmation, Ruby-Spears, and Marvel Productions. Today, the syndication business is a thriving, competitive phenomenon with scores of first-run animated shows, hundreds of new half-hours currently in production, new times, new kids' stations, and a host of toy manufacturers, cereal companies, greeting card makers, and publishers all wanting a piece of the action. The creative community that turned out approximately 200 half-hours of new programming in 1982 will turn out more than 900 half-hours in 1986.

New producers and syndicators have entered the race and found a receptive environment. There is a seemingly insatiable hunger for new animation product. DIC is now a major producer, as is Rankin-Bass, an animation company owned by Lorimar-Telepictures. Nelvana, a Canadian company, is now doing well in the United States. Walt Disney Productions, which traditionally stayed out of the made for television animation market, jumped in with both feet and now makes shows for Saturday morning network and for syndication. In fact, in a syndication market where shows like "He-Man and the Masters of the Universe," "Transformers," and "Ghostbusters" are leading the way, Disney recently ran a trade ad that said, "He-Men were yesterday . . . Robots are today . . . Ghosts may be tomorrow, but . . . Disney is Forever!" This was for a new Disney show for syndication, 65 half-hours entitled "Disney's Duck Tales," featuring many of Disney's timeless and endearing characters.

1. (MUSIC UNDER) ANNCR: (VO) New Autobots

2. join Optimus Prime,

3. Smoke Screen, Tracks,

4. Hoist, Inferno,

5. Red Alert and Grapple.

6. And joining the evil Deceptacons, Thrust and Dirge.

7. CHORUS: Transformers,

8. more than meets the eye.

9. The Transformers.

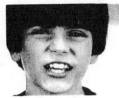

10. BOY 1: (SYNTHESIZED VOICE) Robots in disguise.

11. The Transformers.

12. BOY 2: Deceptacon attack!

13. BOY 3: Autobots will stop 'em.

14. CHORUS: The Transformers.

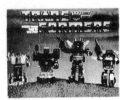

15. ANNCR: (VO) The Transformers, sold separately

16. from Hasbro.

Hasbro's Transformers led the parade of popular robots in the toy industry. The product line and its story of the Autobots versus the Decepticons made for an exciting 65 half-hour syndicated series. (By permission of Griffin Bacal Inc. for Hasbro Inc.)

The new "Thundercats" show from Rankin-Bass is reminiscent of the "He-Man and the Masters of the Universe" show that preceded it. It is now the number one children's show in syndication and will be released as a movie entitled Thundercats Ho! *(By permission of Lorimar-Telepictures)*

At this writing there are 42 children's half-hour animated shows in syndication; five more animated series of such old theatrical cartoons as "Bugs Bunny," "Woody Woodpecker," and "Tom and Jerry" are still in syndication; and 20 more animated series that we know about are currently in production or being offered for sale in syndication. So many new shows have been pumped into the market so quickly that many people are predicting a fallout because of the glut in the marketplace. Stations simply cannot play that much material.

The reasons behind this rather sudden and hot new trend are several. One must understand that the production of an animated half-hour has become very expensive, $200,000 to $300,000 per half-hour. It takes $15 million to $20 million—a substantial financial commitment—to produce 65 first class half-hours of an animated series. The networks have a limited capacity for this type of fare as well as limited budgets, but suddenly, some new windows of financial opportunity have opened up. Toy companies with deep pockets, like Mattel and Hasbro, saw opportunities to popularize a line of toys that could sell in the hundreds of millions with a hit syndicated show. Hence, they risked financing for "He-Man and the Masters of the Universe" and "Transformers," both now running in syndication in more than 80 percent of the country. Mattel, flushed with success, followed "He-Man" with "She-Ra" and Hasbro followed "Transformers" with "G.I. Joe." Other toy companies joined in with "Gobots" and "Mask." On the heels of these successes, more confident production and syndication companies entered the markets with series that could generate millions in licensed toy products, shows such as the number one leading syndicated children's show, "Thundercats" from Rankin-Bass; "Ghostbusters" from Filmation; and "Defenders of the Earth" from King Features/ Marvel Productions.

In addition to revenue gained by selling these libraries to the stations and from the shared royalties from licensed products, other new markets have opened. Canada now pays well for animated series and with so many new stations and delivery systems starting all over the world, a good animated series based on a universal subject can now sell in more than 100 other countries. Today the United States accounts for only 60 percent of the total revenue that a producer and syndicator can obtain from broadcasters on a worldwide sale. And all broadcasters want rerun rights for which they are willing to pay additional fees beyond the first runs.

A common practice today is to edit parts of a half-hour cartoon library into an hour-and-a-half feature motion picture. Animated features have come back into their own and have become respectable products on the world market. A feature length version of "Care Bears" opened up the market with box office sales in the United States of $25 million and that has been followed by *My Little Pony, Transformers,* and *G.I. Joe,* with more titles currently in production.

One would think that children who have seen these programs on television and now in the movies would tire of them, but evidently children want to watch familiar cartoons. These movies are subsequently sold to video cassette companies for even further exposure. More than 500,000 video cassettes of "Transformers" have been sold.

 **1.** (MUSIC UNDER)

 **2.** MAN 1: My brother's in trouble.

 **3.** MAN 2: How do you know? MAN 1: I know.

 **4.** MAN SINGS: Until now Joe's had it easy,

 **5.** but now it's gonna get real hard.

 **6.** Cobra's hired evil twin brothers,

 **7.** leaders of the Crimson Guard.

 **8.** ANNCR: (VO) And here they are, the leaders of the Crimson Guard.

 **9.** The evil twin brothers,

 **10.** Tomax

 **11.** and Zamot

 **12.** and they're getting away in the Cobra Ferret.

 **13.** BOY: The Joe's will stop him.

 **14.** ANNCR: With the G.I. Joe Mini Tank.

 **15.** MEN SING: G.I. Joe...

 **16.** The great American hero. BOYS: Cobra!

 **17.** ANNCR: Evil twin brothers sold together.

 **18.** Cobra Ferret,

 **19.** G.I. Joe Mini Tank and Joe figures sold separately.

20. BOY: (VO) Go, Joe.

Hasbro's GI Joe became such a popular toy it inspired a series of television specials and then a series of 65 half-hours for syndication. (By permission of Griffin Bacal Inc. for Hasbro Inc.)

Cable: A Third Force in Children's Television

Cable television, originally known as CATV (Community Antenna Television), was invented to improve television reception in rural communities either ringed with mountains that blocked signals or located in deep valleys where a microwave signal couldn't penetrate. The story goes that a few local television set retailers, in an effort to sell television sets in their towns, set up a community antenna on the nearest mountain top and then ran cable to the television sets they sold. Legend has it that this type of situation occurred in Pennsylvania and Oregon at about the same time.

CATV improved network and local station reception, but that was about all. The cable running from the antenna to the store (station or system) and then to the viewers' television sets was capable of sending in more signals but the system owner, usually a small, underfinanced entrepreneur, didn't have the resources or the know-how to provide more programming to his subscribers, even though the cable had the capability. Lack of inexpensive programming inhibited the growth of cable in the early years.

The industry was dramatically changed when Home Box Office, a pay-TV company owned by Time Inc., conducted an experiment in which a television signal was bounced off a satellite. The signal moving from the Earth up to a satellite orbiting 25,000 miles overhead was reflected down to cover all of the United States. This method of transmission, rather than the expensive terrestrial microwave signal used by the networks, allowed new programmers to feed a growing body of cable operators with an entirely new spectrum of programming and, within a short period of time, stimulate the wiring of almost half of America.

In 1975, there were almost 70 million television households in the United States. Only 11,136,000 homes (16 percent) were wired for cable television. As large companies entered the business and financed the wiring of communities for cable, the industry grew rapidly. Today there are 87,800,000 television homes in the United States and 39,510,000 (45 percent) of them receive cable television. It is predicted that by 1990 there will be 93,900,000 television homes and 50,706,000 (54 percent) of them will be wired for cable.

The apparent financial opportunities created by the new satellite technology encouraged giant companies to come into the industry to cash in on this new bonanza. Time Inc., Westinghouse, Cox Broadcasting, Warner Communications, Storer, and many others plunged into this new business and poured millions into its development. Getting franchises for new cities and communities became like the Gold Rush. City and community governments, desirous of getting cable for their occupants, were courted by some of the largest companies in American industry. The bidding for valuable franchises was fierce and the city governments were virtually in the position of asking and getting as many as 110 new cable channels added to their subscriber's reception. In addition to the multiplicity of channels demanded, almost every city or community granting a cable franchise insisted upon at least one channel which would provide quality television for children.

NICKELODEON: THE FIRST CHANNEL FOR KIDS

Warner Communications was one of the first companies to buy and develop new cable systems. They quickly discovered that the wiring of America was going to require even greater resources than they, a large entertainment conglomerate, could provide. They formed a 50-50 partnership with American Express, who at that time wanted to expand into the communication business. Undoubtedly they also had visions of consumers participating in electronic home shopping with their American Express Cards.

The joint-venture company, then known as Warner-Amex, was split into two parts: Warner-Amex Cable Communications Inc. and the Warner-Amex Satellite Entertainment Company. One company owned, operated, and developed cable systems and the other created programming and delivered it by satellite to its own and other cable systems. The programming company's first network was a pay-TV movie channel called The Star Channel (later changed to The Movie Channel). It's second network was Nickelodeon which started delivering children's programming to cable operators in 1979. The first programs were some inexpensive shows created at the Warner-owned system in Columbus, Ohio along with some acquired programs from Great Britain and other parts of Europe. At its inception it was not the kind of children's programming that would give either commercial broadcasting or public television any competition.

The chief executive of the new programming company was a seasoned broadcast executive, Jack Schneider. He had a long and brilliant career at CBS and for several years was president of that network. His executive vice-president and chief operating officer was a former protégé at CBS named John Lack. Lack had some experience in the earlier pioneering of cable and together the two men were trying to put together the most dynamic new programming company in the cable industry.

At that time (early 1980), I was working at Ogilvy & Mather in New York as a Senior International Executive looking after several of the agency's largest clients in 24 different countries. For two years I had been living out of a suitcase with a perpetual case of jet lag. On one of my quick pit stops in New York, the Chairman of Ogilvy & Mather asked me to pay a call on one of their new clients in the cable business who was trying to start a new cable network for kids and was sorely in need of some counsel. He asked if I would see Jack Schneider and John Lack and provide whatever advice I could.

I had met Jack only briefly during his days at CBS and with more time was captivated by his style. I was also taken by John Lack's vitality and vision of the future. We had a whirlwind courtship and by mid-year I found myself heading Nickelodeon with the charge to pioneer it and build it into a significant and profitable business—a bright and shining new light in children's television.

Looking back on it, I must say Nickelodeon was an idea that came along at exactly the right time. There had never been a channel exclusively devoted to children's programming. Commercial television in 1979 and 1980 was playing nothing but cartoons and very few shows of quality. Public television was badly in need of funds and had nothing new to offer except remakes of "Sesame Street." CTW had only produced two original shows in ten years. Consumerists were lambasting the networks and commercial stations. New cable operators, anxious to reflect the opinions and desires of their subscribers, were clamoring for a quality children's television product. Beyond that, cable operators had real promises to keep regarding children's programming if their franchises were to be renewed.

I wish I could say with some degree of honesty that it was Warner-Amex's or my own genuine desire to provide better, more inspiring children's programming because of a burning sense of social responsibility or because we felt the country needed it. I can't. I would be kidding myself and you, and would not be able to make the point that Nickelodeon, for all of its lofty aims and subsequent broadcasting awards, was and is a product born of the demands of the marketplace. Very little quality television for children existed. We believed there was a small market for it, and we could fill that void. Beyond that, our customers, the cable operator universe, wanted it, needed it, and would pay for it. They neither wanted nor would pay for the same kind of cartoon programming the commercial broadcasters were using. That would not have been different enough; it would not have added something new and different to the existing broadcast spectrum; and it would not have genuinely fulfilled their obligations to the cities and communities that had granted their franchises.

I must also admit that I would not have taken the position at Nickelodeon if the job had required me to create and produce the same kind of animation programs that have played in commercial broadcasting for the past 30 years. I would have seen no challenge in that nor the opportunity to do something entirely different. It was the chance to manage the first network for kids and do it my own way that prompted me to leave a comfortable 27-year career in the advertising agency business for a pathfinder's job in an industry just being invented.

One of the benefits of managing Nickelodeon was the degree of autonomy I was promised and given. Management's only caveat to me, other than our mutual understanding about the need to do something refreshingly different, was that I was not to spend any more money than our slender budget allowed. While top management at Warner's and American Express examined our financial statements frequently, to my knowledge they never saw a single episode of Nickelodeon. This degree of freedom gave me the opportunity to question and rethink everything that had been done in children's television since its inception. I started with the logotype for the channel and had a signature designed that would become a living thing in video—a logo that could be stretched, pulled apart, blown up, jumped on, and played with in an infinite number of whimsical ways. Instead of using a traditional broadcast on-air look for the network, conventionally a graphic rendition of call letters and a claim, such as, "We're the One," "Proud as a Peacock," and the like, we dispensed with the hype kids didn't care about anyway and developed on-air identifications with catchy music that would be entertaining for children to look at.

Gradually we replaced the original Columbus-produced programming with fresh and original age-specific shows. We refined "Pinwheel," our morning preschool show, into a wonderful electronic sandbox of short pieces that combined puppets, songs, simple mini-dramas, cartoons, and short subjects all geared to help children get along with others and enhance their socialization. We created a new form of sports show for boys and girls and persuaded baseball great Reggie Jackson to host it. The show not only showed championship junior sports events, it interviewed the young participants, coaches, and parents and provided lessons about the life values gained from sports involvement. This show interested all ages.

We discovered a mime and musical group in San Francisco that acted out letters from children and developed a show around them called "Kid's Writes." "Livewire," a Phil Donahue-type talk and variety show for teens was created and we found a talented, unknown host, Fred Newman, who subsequently became one of cable's first celebrities. We created a show to

Nickelodeon's "Pinwheel" show combines puppets, songs, mini-dramas, cartoons, and other short subjects into a pro-social electronic sandbox for preschoolers. (By permission of MTV Networks, Inc.)

Host Fred Newman discusses relevant teen topics with the audience on Nickelodeon's "Livewire," a Phil Donahue-type show for young teenagers. (By permission of MTV Networks, Inc.)

Don Herbert, the original "Mr. Wizard" seen on NBC for 16 years, is brought back to television in a new up-to-date format created by Nickelodeon. "Mr. Wizard" continues to perform his magical scientific experiments which combine entertainment and education for children. (By permission of MTV Networks, Inc.)

Host Leonard Nimoy of "Star Trek" fame takes young viewers behind the scenes to show them how movies are made. The show reveals the secrets of stunts, makeup, special effects, and other movie-making techniques and shows excerpts from forthcoming movies. (By permission of MTV Networks, Inc.)

take children behind the scenes in the making of movies. Leonard Nimoy of "Star Trek" hosted this show called "Standby . . .Lights! Camera! Action!" Bill Bixby, who children knew from his roles on "My Favorite Martian," "Eddie's Father," and "The Magician" joined our network to host our juvenile biography show, "Against the Odds." We brought "Mr. Wizard" back to television. Don Herbert had his "Mr. Wizard" science show for children on NBC for 16 years. We found Don active and busy with science projects in California and developed a new 1980s format for him to perform his famous experiments on the air again.

Our needs for comedy were served by a "Laugh-In" type show for kids produced by Roger Price in Canada. Price's "You Can't Do That on Television" became one of Nickelodeon's most popular properties. We also found and acquired such wonderful family shows as "The Adventures of Black Beauty" and a futuristic adventure show that had been number one with kids in England called "The Tomorrow People."

We created and put together a variety of shows for children of all ages that television had not seen before. While we played some occasional cartoons, none of them were violent and more importantly, they did not look like what children were seeing on commercial broadcasts. Even our television commercials encouraging children to watch the channel were done differently. We found an artist in Portland, Oregon, Will Vinton, who had won an Academy Award nomination for his short subject done in "Claymation" and asked him to do our commercials in his magical technique using animated clay forms. We were the first advertiser to use him for a television commercial.

Our efforts did not go unnoticed. Television critics were unanimous in their praise. The critic of New York's *Village Voice,* who was known to hate television in general, said Nickelodeon was one of the best things on the air. Bob Matteo of *Cablevision* magazine said Nickelodeon had created the "finest body of children's programming on television." We received awards from every competition cable programming could enter. Most significant of all, in 1983 we became the first cable channel to receive the George Foster Peabody award, the Pulitzer prize of Broadcasting. Nothing out of cable television has won it since.

Most of this programming, created from 1980 to 1984, is still on Nickelodeon today. *TV Guide* (February 15, 1986) published one of its occasional articles listing the best children's shows on television as voted by network executives, children's educators, consumer advocates, clinical psychologists, and pediatricians. Of 18 children's shows mentioned, five were among the aforementioned group of shows we created at Nickelode-

1. CLAYMATION MAN 1: You probably think Nickelodeon is a channel...

2. CLAYMATION MAN 2: ...for little kids. Well, it is...until the big kids get home.

3. (MUSIC) CLAYMATION MAN 1: Then it changes

4. into a channel of Rock concerts (MUSIC STOPS)

5. and interviews, (SFX: APPLAUSE)

6. behind the scenes movie previews

7. and some great comedy. (SFX: BUZZER)

8. So even if you thought Nickelodeon...

9. CLAYMATION KIDS: was for little kids...

10. CLAYMATION MAN 1: that doesn't mean you can't...

11. (SFX) change your mind.

12. (SFX) Nickelodeon on your local cable channel. (SFX)

Nickelodeon did unusual commercials to promote increased viewing of the channel. They were the first to use academy award-winning claymation artist, Will Vinton, for television commercials for children. (By permission of MTV Networks, Inc.)

on in those years: "Pinwheel"; "Standby . . . Lights! Camera! Action!"; "Mr. Wizard's World"; our teen show, "Livewire"; and "You Can't Do That on Television."

As Nickelodeon's rapid growth was spurred by this new form of children's television, other cable networks decided to put some children's shows on the air. WTBS, the superstation, was already playing what other children's stations were playing. The USA Network added two children's time-blocks. The Christian Broadcast Network played children's shows with pro-social overtones. Even the pay-movie channels added children's fare to their schedules, HBO with Jim Henson's "Fraggle Rock" and Showtime with "Faerie Tale Theatre." By the end of 1983, the combined cable networks were playing more of what I thought was better programming than the networks.

When, in a speech to the New York Ad Club, I claimed that cable had more and better programming than the networks did, that comment was not taken well by at least one network executive in charge of children's programming. Squire Rushnell of ABC, who has been one of the most conscientious and dedicated of all the children's programming executives in the past 30 years, took offense at my remarks and felt I was flinging down the gauntlet. He wrote me an agitated letter challenging my statement and saw fit to copy six other executives at ABC. I answered him on January 26, 1984, with the following letter:

Mr. Squire D. Rushnell
ABC Entertainment
1330 Avenue of the Americas
New York, New York 10019

Dear Mr. Rushnell:

I am sorry you feel compelled to challenge my statement regarding children's programming on cable vs. the networks. The statement was not made in the spirit of a "duel at dawn" or flinging a gauntlet. It was made to prove a point.

We, and everyone else in our industry, use the networks as the gold standard. For cable to do anything more or better than the networks is a rare and unusual achievement . . . and that's all I was saying.

The remark was used in the following context in a speech I gave to the New York Ad Club.

Nickelodeon has more original, first-time U.S. view kids' programming in one day than the networks have in one week. It is also both interesting and gratifying to note that the rest of cable television has since taken an interest in quality television for children as well ... HBO with their "Fraggle Rock" series; Showtime with their outstanding "Faerie Tale Theater"; USA with "Calliope," "Co-Ed" and "Sports Academy"; and the Disney Channel with several new shows for children, all comprise a new body of original children's programming which hasn't been available in commercial broadcasting for two and a half decades. *Children's programming is one of the few areas where cable has already passed the networks.*

You challenged the veracity of this statement. Attached please find a breakdown of the shows and number of hours for children currently being aired by the various cable services. Total hours per week: 162.5.

I hardly think we have any argument about quantity.

I would be last to claim "quality" for *all* the shows on cable. The ones I cited in my talk are the ones I admire most. Perhaps you'd have some problems with our definition of "quality shows," but your mention of CTW, NBC's *Project Peacock* or CBS' *In the News*, leads me to believe we are talking about the same thing.

Frankly, I am not as horrified by your Saturday morning cartoon lineups as you might think. Lord knows, I have bought enough time in them during my career, and even sold your network a couple of my own. But, I do believe there is a stultifying sameness to the cartoon entertainment on television and all the networks should be reaching out more often for something more.

As for Nickelodeon and our commitments versus your own, please make your own comparisons. Our shows are trying to be an alternative to the bulk of cartoon fare on commercial television. Our shows strive to entertain first ... but to also provide something more substantive in the way of information, positive social values, positive role models, literary values, etc. You might say that would be our definition of quality programming for kids.

For your comparative purposes, here's a general breakdown of what we've been playing 14 hours a day, 7 days a week.

All of the following is first time U.S. view programming (except where noted) and much of it is original programming created exclusively for Nickelodeon:

1) PINWHEEL
   260 hours ... pre-school

2) TODAY's SPECIAL
   39 half hours ... pre-school

3) WHAT WILL THEY THINK OF NEXT
   100 half hours - science

4) KIDS' WRITES
   17 half hours - performances of kid's creative material

5) YOU CAN'T DO THAT ON TELEVISION
   39 half-hours (26 more in production) - comedy

6) GOING GREAT
   39 half hours - kid's documentary

7) BLACK BEAUTY
   52 half hours (26 of these are first time U.S. view) - drama

8) THIRD EYE
   28 half hours - drama

9) AGAINST THE ODDS
   26 half hours - juvenile biography

10) TOMORROW PEOPLE - 68 half hours - drama

11) LIVEWIRE
    139 half hours - teen talk and variety

12) MR. WIZARD
    26 half hours - science

All of the above shows air in any given weekday. The following air weekends only:

1) REGGIE JACKSON'S WORLD OF SPORTS
   18 hours - sports

2) STANDBY ... LIGHTS! CAMERA! ACTION!
   13 hours - about the movies

In addition, we play specials every weekend and short films throughout the week.

I hope I have adequately addressed your challenge of my remarks. Again ... I had no desire to set up a duel ... but I don't think I have overstated the facts.

Sincerely,

CS:nw

cc: Sy Amlen, Mike Dann, Lew Erlicht, Herb Granath, Al Schneider, John Severino - ABC

The Problems with Cable Television

The growth of cable has been tremendous, but it is still only available in approximately 45 percent of America's television households. In addition, very little programming on cable is attracting large audiences by conventional broadcast standards.

HBO, the largest of the pay-TV channels, occasionally gets a large audience for a popular movie, but none of the basic channels that broadcast news, sports, financial news, cultural programming, video music, and children's shows are attracting a large audience on a regular basis. Hence, cable is limited as an advertising medium and advertisers are not pouring hundreds of millions into cable to support it. For most television advertisers, cable is an afterthought.

Nielsen ratings for cable are a little foggy because of the size of the cable sample. For example, the Nielsen metered ratings for all television are taken from 1,700 television homes. Only about 675 of those homes have cable. Making matters worse in trying to determine the ratings for children's shows is that only 35 percent of the 1,700 home sample have children under 11 years old. This, of course, makes the measured children's homes sample even smaller.

Just to provide some quantitative perspective, Nickelodeon is one of the best rated of all basic cable channels. December 1986 ratings show an average of 1.0 during daytime hours. Even though approximately 30 million homes have the capability to receive Nickelodeon today, the ratings indicate that about 250,000 children are watching at any one time. That number is almost insignificant compared to an average show on Saturday morning network which reaches more than three million children. Advertisers could probably reach more than 250,000 children with a single commercial on a high-rated children's program on commercial stations in New York and Los Angeles alone.

Because of the small audience, cable cannot command high advertising rates. That and the enormous expense of wiring the cities is holding back the growth of the medium. Programmers need revenue to continue to produce new material. They simply cannot afford a continual flow of it against today's high production costs. Nickelodeon, for example, was recently purchased along with MTV and VH-1 from Warner-Amex by Viacom. The group was sold, along with their libraries, for $450 million. It will probably be a long while before Viacom will recover its costs, if ever. Consequently, very little new production money is being poured into Nickelodeon and the channel has started to rerun such ancients as "The Donna Reed Show," "Lassie," and "Dennis the Menace." They need the reruns to fill the broadcast hours and this material is available and cheap, but it will not continue to hold an audience in the long run. Large and regular television audiences are obtained by fresh, original programming, and kids are no exception. They'll watch more reruns than adults if they like the material, but even they grow tired eventually. Viacom will have to invest in new production if Nickelodeon is to survive in the years to come.

The VCR Revolution

In addition to more broadcast television than ever before, the viewer's options for video entertainment have now been widened by the advent of the video cassette recorder. Viewers can now watch what they want to watch when they want to watch it. If a parent and child want to see a particular show at a time when they will not be at home, they can tape it and watch it at a more convenient hour. Programs can be rented or purchased from retail outlets to be seen over and over again.

There are already 22 million VCRs in the United States and experts are predicting that 50 percent of all homes will have a VCR unit by the early 1990s. One of the most interesting aspects of the growth of the VCR is the importance of children's programming.

At this time the market is dominated by feature motion picture rentals, but in terms of rental and purchase of video cassettes, children's programming has become the second largest selling category. In dollar volume, children's programs grew from 8.75 percent of the total in 1983 to 11 percent in 1984 and approximately 13 percent in 1985 and climbing. One reputable report indicates that the children's video market generated sales of 12 million units and a wholesale volume of $210 million in 1985.

It is more than apparent that the VCR revolution will continue to play an important role in becoming part of children's viewing diets. Parents and children are enjoying the new convenience and selectivity of this medium, and families are beginning to collect cassettes like they once collected books for a home library. Favorite programs can be passed from child to child in larger families.

FUTURE DEVELOPMENTS IN CHILDREN'S ADVERTISING

One of the questions surrounding the new VCR medium is whether or not it will become an advertising medium. It is easy to conceive, for example, of a toy company-generated program on cassette including an info-mercial at the beginning or end of the program. Already certain liquor advertisers are sponsoring bartenders guides in video form and airlines are backing travel cassettes with shows about their key destinations. This opportunity is open to any large advertiser who can formulate his message into a how-to or entertainment form.

I, for one, believe advertising will become part of children's cassettes before we enter the '90s. I believe we will see a new long-form, information-packed type of television commercial in children's cassettes—advertising in an entirely different tone.

Along the same lines, I believe we will begin to see more and more experimentation with 15-second commercials for children. Broadcasters are already accepting them for adult products and a handful of advertisers are turning to the use of back-to-back 15s to comprise a 30-second commercial. If children's advertisers learn that a 15-second commercial can truly communicate to children almost as much as a 30-second commercial, they will begin to use them. This applies most particularly to the toy companies who have long lines of products to sell and need sufficient air time to expose them all.

INTERACTIVE TELEVISION

The buzzword at the February 1987 New York Toy Fair was *interactive* television. Mattel and Axlon Toys introduced two interactive shows that, they claimed, represent the next trend in children's television. Both Mattel's "Captain Power" and Axlon's "Moto Monsters and the Tech-force" were touted as new weekly half-hour programs scheduled to debut in the fall of 1987. Both shows emit inaudible signals that permit viewers to participate by responding to on-screen targets with shooting toys. The

Captain Power toy, for example, is a spaceship that can register hits on an on-screen figure. Mattel's spaceship will sell for approximately $30 while Axlon's radio-controlled, computer-programmable toy will retail for about $250. Both companies insist that owning the toy is not a prerequisite to enjoying the television shows.

Undoubtedly, most people have forgotten that this is not broadcasting's first experiment with interactive television. In 1953 Jack Berry, Dan Enright, and Ed Friendly developed an interactive children's show called "Winky Dink and You" which premiered on CBS on Saturday, October 10th. The key to really enjoying the show was the Winky Dink Magic TV Kit that sold for 50 cents. The kit provided a sheet of clear acetate that would attach to a television screen. Youngsters could then draw on the set and thus participate in the show's storytelling. The producers sold millions of the kits and the show was on for four and a half years even though its ratings were only fair. Eventually it was swamped by the competition of straight cartoon shows.

It is doubtful that the new interactive shows will do as well. For one thing, the kids audience of today is too jaded to be taken in for too long by a gimmick. The shows will be taped in the affluent houses that can afford the toys and are most likely to have a VCR. The taped shows will then be used to play with the toys in the same fashion as electronic games. As the interest in scoring hits off the screen quickly wanes, the toys and the tapes will end up in the closet with the electronic games of a few seasons ago. The kids will then return to the newest of the cartoon shows that will captivate their imaginations.

WHAT'S A PARENT TO DO?

With all the new options for television viewing for children, children will continue to watch as much television as ever, if not more. What should concerned parents do with this plethora of video entertainment for their children? The problem, which has always been a vexing one, has now grown to highly complicated proportions.

The extremist position, of course, is held by those who believe television is harmful to children. There is no answer for this group nor is there any compromise. These people must either disconnect the television set or throw it out of the home.

There is a more moderate position saying that only some television is harmful to children. These parents must monitor all their child's television viewing and limit it to those programs which they know are acceptable. The VCR should be very helpful to these families.

Obviously, both of these groups represent minority positions in the total number of families with children under 12.

For the majority of families, equally concerned but reluctant or unable to monitor or limit their children's viewing patterns, I have some suggestions:

- Watch television with your children. Discuss what you have seen and explain difficult issues.
- Learn more about the medium and its limitations. It will make you more tolerant of its failings and wise enough to explain what's going on to your children.
- Use the medium conscientiously. Seek out shows your children will enjoy, and shows that help their process of socialization. Don't be surprised if some of these shows are cartoons.
- Limit the viewing of children. Too much of any one thing for a child under 12 cannot be healthy or productive.
- Strictly monitor that which you object to. Simply change the channel to something more acceptable or turn the set off for the time being. Direct the child to another activity.

I clearly want to make the point that if you can't whip 'em, join 'em. I believe it is possible to take the best parts of children's television and use them constructively. It is possible to see beyond the junk aspects of it to a useful popular culture and interpret its meanings in constructive ways with your child.

Even Peggy Charren has come around to that point of view. ACT has a new campaign with the theme "Get TV Smart." ACT maintains that parents have both the power and obligation to improve their child's television habits. Peggy Charren has been recently quoted as saying, "If families sit down together and talk about television, they can figure out what TV does well and what it does badly."

Beyond television, other forces in our culture outside the home are accelerating the role of children as consumers. The fragmentation of the nuclear family, day-care centers, nursery schools, and babysitters all play a role in influencing younger children's tastes and wants. New teenage freedom and fashions are influencing the subteens. Television, used wisely and judiciously, can help your child cope with his or her growing responsibility as a consumer.

Afterword

OBVIOUSLY, I FEEL THERE IS VALUE IN CHILDREN'S TELEVISION. I SEE NO REASON to maintain the melancholy pretense of absolute objectivity. I like my work very much and am no doubt biased in its favor. I am not blind to the failings of children's television, but like many of us who have paid attention to the predicament, I have done what I could to find intelligent solutions while television itself was trying to find its bearings.

Still, I would like the dissenters of children's television to know that mine is a noncombatant point of view. I feel no need to apologize or champion what I have done. Neither will I take sides against what other children's television practitioners have done because that would be taking sides against myself. I simply hope that the battle over children's television will end because there will no longer be any need for the battle to continue. Since the battle is now at a stalemate, it is a good time to review.

For those practitioners or students of communication who have found my comments useful, I ask you to take your responsibility with the children's audience seriously. Communicate with them honestly and fairly. Be sensitive to their needs and wants. Recognize that certain behavior seen on television is imitated. Understand that the consumer isn't just a bunch of unruly kids out there waiting to react to the next fad. The consumer is your own child or your friend's child. And that consumer must be treated with the same respect, judgment, and restraint you would try to exercise with your own child or anyone else in your family.

It's only good sense—and good business.

Select Bibliography

Books

Barcus, F. Earle. *Children's Television: An Analysis of Programming and Advertising*. New York: Praeger Publishers, 1977.

Barnouw, Erik. *The Tube of Plenty*. New York: Oxford University Press, 1975.

Bower, Robert T. *Television and the Public*. New York: Holt, Rinehart, and Winston, 1973.

Bower, Robert T. *The Changing Television Audience in America*. New York: Columbia University Press, 1985.

Brown, Les. *Encyclopedia of Television*. New York: Quadrangle/The New York Times Book Company, 1977.

Brown, Les. *Television: The Business Behind the Box*. New York: Harcourt Brace Jovanovich, Inc., 1971.

Fischer, Stuart. *Kid's TV the First 25 Years*. New York: Facton File Publications, 1983.

Gerber, George et al. *Violence Profile No. 8*. Philadelphia: Annenberg School of Communications, University of Pennsylvania, 1977.

Grossman, Gary H. *Saturday Morning TV*. New York: Dell Publishing Co., 1981.

Helitzer, Mel. *The Youth Market*. New York: Media Books, 1970.

Johnson, Nicholas. *How To Talk Back To Your Television Set*. Boston: Little, Brown and Company, 1970.

Kaye, Evelyn. *The ACT Guide to Children's Television*. Boston: Beacon Press, 1979.

Mayer, Martin. *About Television*. New York: Harper & Row, 1972.

Melody, William H. *Children's Television: The Economics of Exploitation*. New Haven: Yale University Press, 1973.

Moody, Kate. *Growing Up on Television*. New York: The New York This Book Company, 1980.

Schramm, Wilbur; Lyle, Jack; and Parker, Edwin B. *Television in the Lives of Our Children.* Stanford: Stanford University Press, 1961.

Steiner, Gary A. *The People Look at Telvision.* New York: Knopf, 1962.

Ward, Scott; Wachnam, Daniel B.; and Wartella, Ellen. *How Children Learn to Buy.* Beverly Hills, California: Sage Publications, 1977.

Winn, Marie. *The Plug-In Drug.* New York: Viking Press, 1977.

Woolry, George W. *Children's Television: The First Thirty-Five Years, 1946-1981.* Vol. I and Vol. II Metuchen, New Jersey & London: The Scarecrow Press, Inc., 1983 and 1985.

ARTICLES

Bogart, Leo. "Warning: The Surgeon General Has Determined that TV Violence is Moderately Dangerous to Your Child's Mental Health." *The Public Opinion Quarterly* 36 (Winter 1972-1973).

Leifer, Aimee Dorr; Gordon, Neal J.; and Graves, Sheryl Browne. "Children's Television: More than Mere Entertainment." *Harvard Educational Review* 44:2 (1976).

Ward, Scott. "Kids TV—Marketers on the Hot Seat." *The Commercial Connection* New York: Dell Publishing Co., Inc., 1979.

Ward, Scott. "Compromise in Commercials for Children." *Harvard Business Review* 56:6 (November-December 1978).

Wells, William D."Communicating with Children." *Journal of Advertising Research* (June 1965).

Zoglin, Richard. "The Coming Battle Over TV Ads for Kids." *The Commercial Connection.* New York: Dell Publishing Co., Inc., 1979.

Index

About the Author

FEW PEOPLE ARE AS QUALIFIED TO WRITE A DEFINITIVE BOOK ABOUT CHILDREN'S television as Cy Schneider. For the past 32 years he has worked in almost every phase of the medium.

Beginning in 1953 at the Carson/Roberts advertising agency in Los Angeles, he was the first copy-contact person on the then tiny Mattel account. For the next 26 years he stayed with the account, and under his advertising stewardship, Mattel became the world's largest toy maker, with sales increasing from $4 million to more than $300 million annually.

During those years Schneider wrote, directed, or supervised the creation of more than 1,000 kid's commercials for more than 400 different products. Notably, he conceived and wrote the first commercials for the Barbie doll, Chatty Cathy, the Fanner 50, Agent Zero M toys, and many more. He was also intimately involved in the creation and production of such Mattel sponsored television shows as "Matty's Funday Funnies," "The Funny Company," and "Beany and Cecil."

In 1965 Schneider became President of Carson/Roberts and continued in that post when the agency was acquired by Ogilvy & Mather in 1970. While with Ogilvy & Mather, Schneider worked on the children's advertising for General Foods' Kool-Aid, Burger Chef stores, and Post Cereals. He was also involved in the development of television plans and children's commercials for Hersheys, Ralston Cereals, Universal Studios, Del Monte, Lever, Baskin-Robbins 31 Flavors, and various other chewing gum, candy, beverage, and toy brands in many other countries throughout the world. He has worked in virtually every product category for children and in almost every country where children's television exists.

Schneider left Ogilvy & Mather in 1980 to work for the Warner-Amex Satellite Entertainment Company where he pioneered the development and growth of Nickelodeon, the first cable network for kids. Under his management the network grew from scratch to more than 20 million subscribers and its quality programming for children won evey major award offered by the broadcast industry. In 1983 Nickelodeon was the first cable channel to receive the "Pulitzer prize of broadcasting," the coveted Peabody Award.

In 1984, after six years in New York with Ogilvy and Warner-Amex, Schneider returned to his native Los Angeles where he currently serves as Chairman of the Pacific Division of the Bozell, Jacobs, Kenyon & Eckhardt advertising agency.

Other highlights in Schneider's career include being President of the Southern California 4 A's, Chairman of Western Regional 4 A's, and being elected "The Advertising Man of the Year" in 1975 by the Western States Advertising Agency Association.

He is a graduate of the University of Southern California School of Journalism and holds a Master's Degree in Contemporary American literature from New York University. He served in the United States Army as a parachutist and gliderman with the 11th Airborne Division in the Pacific. He is married and has 5 children.